"The question at the heart of this book is one I've studied all my life: What is leadership? I've met leaders in many areas—healthcare, community revitalization, education—and find Chris's thoughts on the subject compelling. I love that he starts with self-mastery. Before one can help others, they must get their own insides right. I love that the next piece is caring for others. The rest of the book naturally flows from these two powerful acts. Finally, I love that this book is also a workbook. Chris walks us through his framework while encouraging us to think, journal, envision, and keep doing the unending (lifelong) work of learning to be a leader."

Quint Studer,
Author of *The Calling: Why Healthcare Is So Special*

"*The Anatomy of Leadership* is one of the most innovative and entertaining books on leadership I have read in years. Just when I thought everything about leadership had been written and said, along comes an author with a fresh perspective and a very timely message. In the pages of this book, author Chris Comeaux goes deep into the true meaning and impact of leadership and gives his readers the tools and strategies that can greatly expand their leadership thinking and growth. No matter where you are on your leadership journey, this book is one to put at the top of your list."

Meridith Elliott Powell, Business Growth Strategist, Award-Winning Author of *Thrive,* **Hall of Fame Speaker**

"Chris and I have been friends for more than four decades now. He was a learner way back then, and *The Anatomy of Leadership* demonstrates that he's still a deep thinker. In his book, Chris has translated his knowledge and its application to his own career as an executive to teaching. He takes the best of the best nuggets from all his direct mentorship advice and leadership studies to challenge us to broaden our concepts of leadership. He then provides a step-by-step guide to help us personally drive success within our own organizations."

Dawn F. Landry, Author of *Armored* and CEO & Founder, Authentizity, LLC

"If you desire to have an organization composed of high performers living their purpose, then this is a must-read. Out of all the books on leadership, this is by far the most comprehensive, compelling, connective, and clear book that exists. Organizations that have employed Chris' wisdom have truly reached unimaginable levels of excellence. If you are looking to transform your organization's culture, fulfill your mission, and advance your vision, then begin reading *The Anatomy of Leadership* with your entire leadership team today."

Dr. Millicent Burke-Sinclair, Ed.D, MBA, MLAS, SPHR ®, SHRM-SCP, Four Seasons President and CEO

"*The Anatomy of Leadership: What is Leadership and What Do Leaders Do* by Chris Comeaux is a must-read for anyone interested in being a good, purpose-driven leader. I was lucky enough to read an early draft of the book, and Chris graciously allowed me to use a portion of that draft as a text in my undergraduate Leadership Theory & Practice course. Comeaux's work fits that perfect niche of a leader writing from his own experience yet informed by a study of expert leadership principles.

Like his mentor, Dr. Lee Thayer, Comeaux wants to push the reader to self-exploration and deep engagement with the ideas and actions of leadership. Unlike Thayer, however, Comeaux has created a memorable framework that breaks down complex concepts into easily understandable pieces. This isn't a philosophical treatise but an interactive workbook. Comeaux provides a straightforward introduction to each element of his framework and provides humorous and concrete examples and insight from leadership experts. But Comeaux then offers insightful questions to push the reader to dig deeper and find additional layers of meaning and lessons to apply in their own lives and organizations.

Comeaux's writing style is engaging and clear, and his examples and anecdotes make the book relatable and accessible to anyone. Whether you're a seasoned leader or just starting on your leadership journey, *The Anatomy of Leadership* will provide you with valuable insights and practical guidance to help you become a more effective and impactful leader. I highly recommend it!

> **Dr. Marie F. Jones, Professor of Business and Organizational Leadership, Brevard College and author of *To Be the Best by any Measure: Creating & Sustaining a High Performance Organization***

"Chris Comeaux has written a must-read for anyone interested in being a better leader! *The Anatomy of Leadership* presents a wonderful framework for leaders to access their current leadership attributes to become better leaders. Thought-provoking questions throughout the book encourage us to probe the current realities of ourselves and our organizations while outlining a path to living our *cause and purpose*."

> **Bill McKibbin, President, Henderson Oil Company**

"Through his formal studies, his hands-on experience, and his extensive reading and research, Chris Comeaux has evolved a unique and comprehensive view of leadership, particularly as it pertains to mission-driven organizations. *The Anatomy of Leadership* is Chris' way of *paying it forward* to current and future leaders who desire to make a difference in the lives of their employees, customers/clients, and the communities they are privileged to serve. As a combination guidebook and workbook, *The Anatomy of Leadership* meets readers' needs, whether they're looking for a conceptual framework or a step-by-step how-to."

> **Mark B. Cohen, Editor & Publisher *Hospice News Today***

"It does not matter if you are a veteran of leadership or new to the game; Chris Comeaux's deep dive into what makes a great leader is a valuable and worthwhile read. *The Anatomy of Leadership* is a step-by-step guide to improving your leadership skills."

J Darrell Johnson, Senior Vice President, First Horizon Bank

"This two-part book offers common language, valuable lessons learned, thought-provoking questions, and stories for anyone striving toward self-mastery. Regardless of your role in an organization and life, by reading this book, applying the principles, and believing in your ability to drive positive change and outcomes, you can change the world!"

D'Ann Grell, Retired, Global Business Executive, Fortune 500 Company and Vice Chair, Teleios Collaborative Network Board of Directors

"*The Anatomy of Leadership* reader will be challenged to explore new leadership principles and strategies while being inspired to implement extremely practical tools. Chris Comeaux's lifelong passion for leadership development, combined with his years of study with Stephen Covey's mentor, Dr. Lee Thayer, has created an easy-to-use roadmap for all who strive to excel as leaders."

John Locke PCC MBA, Executive Coach, Forvis

"If you have never had the pleasure of having a coffee and a conversation with Chris Comeaux, this book is the next best thing! It is full of practical wisdom, useful information, and leadership lessons from someone who has obviously devoted his life to leadership learning. Thanks to Chris for this workbook to support our next generation (and ourselves) on the journey to self-mastery as leaders and humans."

Julie Kennedy Oehlert, the Chief Experience and Brand Officer at ECU Health

THE ANATOMY OF LEADERSHIP

What is Leadership and What Do Leaders Do?

CHRIS COMEAUX

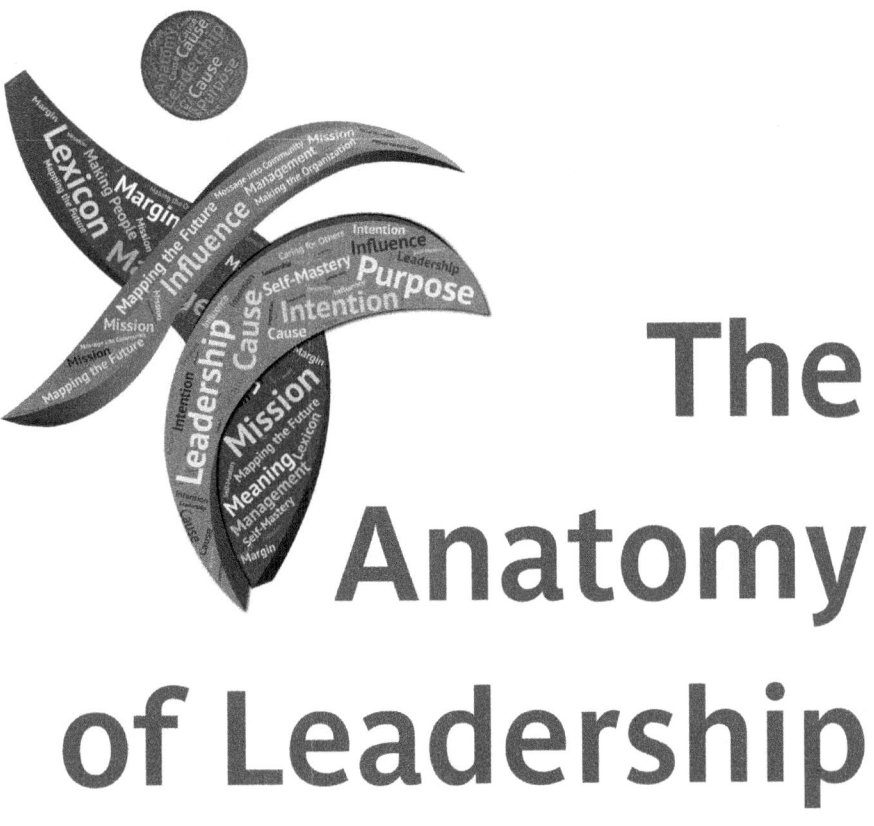

The Anatomy of Leadership

What Is Leadership
And What Do Leaders Do?

Copyright © 2023 Chris Comeaux, No. TX 9-348-393

All rights reserved. No part of this book may be reproduced in any form or by any electronic or mechanical means, including information storage and retrieval systems, without permission in writing from the publisher, except by reviewers, who may quote brief passages in a review.

Paperback: ISBN 979-8-9893304-0-9

First paperback edition: November 2023

Book design and editing: Markind, LLC

Cover Art: Evangeline Comeaux, Jeff Haffner, and Teleios Consulting Group

Printed in the United States of America

Publisher: Teleios Consulting Group, Flat Rock, North Carolina

Website: https://teleioscg.com/anatomy-of-leadership

Dedication

Deshia, my wife, my love, my friend, and my life adventure partner, thank you for being the wind beneath my wings.

To our five amazing children: Ian, Gage, Declan, Ava, and Evangeline. I am so proud of each of you. Continue to believe, and you can do all things.

To Granddaddy, aka Pop, thank you for always seeing in me what I did not see in myself. You have been pushing me to write a book for twenty-eight years. Well, it's now done. Thanks for being such an encourager.

To Dr. Lee Thayer's family: Lee has had a significant impact on my life and contributed to the most intense learning I have ever experienced. I pray this honors and expands much of what he taught.

To Quint Studer: Thank you for showing me the way and pouring into so many of us. You are the Nick Saban of healthcare leaders.

I dedicate this to all the incredible hospice and palliative care team members doing great work as they walk on the sacred ground that is serious illness care every day. I have learned much from many of you.

Thank you, Lord, for purpose and grace to live it every day.

Contents

Introduction 1

PART I - The Anatomy

Chapter One: Self-Mastery 7

Chapter Two: Caring for Others 29

Chapter Three: Influence 43

Chapter Four: Intention 55

Chapter Five: Cause and Purpose 73

Chapter Six: Transition (SCII C&P) 89

PART II - The 7 M's

Chapter Seven: Introduction to the 7 M's 95

Chapter Eight: Mission 99

Chapter Nine: Margin 121

Chapter Ten: Meaning Management 135

Chapter Eleven: Message into the Community 157

Chapter Twelve: Making the Organization 169

Chapter Thirteen: Making People 185

Chapter Fourteen: Mapping the Future 199

Conclusion 221

Appendix 1: Learning Plan Example 233

Appendix 2: Role Description Example 235

Appendix 3: Operational Plan Example 237

Acknowledgments 239

Bibliography 243

Book Preview: *It's About Time* 251

About the Author 263

Foreword

I first had the pleasure of meeting Chris Comeaux at a conference in New York City during the fall of 2006, and even after seventeen years, I vividly remember that moment and the profound impact Chris had on me. During the conference, Chris was promoting his executive coaching services designed for leaders navigating challenging headwinds—offering a different perspective to leadership than the standard *recipe-oriented* solutions I and so many others had grown accustomed to. Chris quickly earned my respect through his unique ability to drive understanding and acceptance that there might be a less conventional—yet better way to achieve success.

At that time, I was a newly appointed CEO of a well-respected not-for-profit hospice and palliative care organization. I was charged with leading organizational transformation—a task I quickly realized was impeded by a culture of resistance to change. Chaos, confusion, and even resentment for change ensued, right down to the types of snacks in the staff vending machine. As somebody who was looking to grow their competencies while actively avoiding *flavor of the week* type programs to fix these issues, Chris truly became a breath of fresh air.

Through the years, Chris and I have developed a strong collegial friendship that has proven beneficial in our work together. He has served as a mentor, a confidante, and a trusted advisor to me on many fronts, and I have witnessed firsthand his passion for helping others learn new talents and live their cause and purpose.

Where others may overcomplicate the purpose of leadership, Chris Comeaux provides a practical and unintimidating approach to solving complex problems. He has a keen ability that takes him straight to the essence of connecting all aspects of an organization with strategic purpose.

While success is conventionally measured by a strong financial bottom line, Chris understands that there is a deeper cut in what contributes to a successful organization. He has masterfully and succinctly written this book to be wonderfully and purposefully unconventional. Influenced by our shared mentor, Dr. Lee Thayer, Chris has an exceptional grasp on this approach—you see, Dr. Thayer taught us that a conventional approach will only produce a conventional result.

Regardless of where you are in *your* stage of leadership, this book will provide insight into connecting the dots of competency, mastery, and virtuosity. This is not just a book; this is a guidepost for you to achieve greatness, a guidepost that is written as a book and workbook together. It really does not get better than this!

Take this book seriously, for it will serve you well. It will be a thought-provoking guide for ongoing insights, practical applications,

Foreword

and the mastery of leadership. You will learn to be a great leader, one who must change the course of all things important to your cause. *The Anatomy of Leadership*, written by Chris Comeaux, wholeheartedly changes the course of things!

**Carole Fisher,
President, National Partnership for Healthcare and Hospice Innovation Senior Advisor, Healthsperien Executive Coach, Speaker and Podcaster**

Preface

Several years ago, I engaged a past team member to return to the organization where I was CEO and perform an assessment. It was a great opportunity, as it was someone who knew us well. He brought a fresh perspective, and we learned many things from the assessment. His most impactful revelation was the observation that we did not have one common definition of leadership, even though leadership is one of the most important principles we espoused. A robust lexicon, a set of verbal tools an organization uses to manage the meaning of things, is critical for an organization's success. Without a defined lexicon, there is a good chance cats will abound.

> **When Cats Abound**
>
> Years ago, a wonderful nurse I worked with taught me what she called *the cat analogy*. If I say the word cat you and I will both nod our heads, believing we have the same understanding. However, you are thinking Calico, and I am thinking Persian.
>
> People may think they are talking about the same thing, but without a lexicon, they may be on different wavelengths. A lexicon is an attempt to prevent the cats from abounding, and when it comes down to such an important topic as leadership, you must have a common definition in your organization. If not, cats will abound, and everyone will struggle to pull in the same direction.

The Anatomy of Leadership

I faced the exact dilemma that I often caution other organizations about. Life is funny that way. It felt like a major mountain to climb, but I was thankful that a key organizational challenge had been identified.

We began a discussion and debate centered around the question, "What is this thing called leadership?" We also asked, "If we created a common definition of leadership, what would it be, and what steps should we take to find the answer?"

While this was occurring, I was providentially completing my Master in Leadership course at The Thayer Institute. The Institute's namesake, Dr. Lee Thayer, spent his life thinking and writing about leadership. Dr. Thayer rarely distilled anything into easy-to-understand pieces. That was part of his charm as he thought deeply and wrote provocatively about things. So I asked him if he had ever tried to distill leadership down to a definition. I have included his response on the next page.

Dr. Thayer challenged his students to think and question things even if it meant making us angry. He once said to us, "There were only three leaders over the 20th Century: Mao, Stalin, and Hitler." Now, those three combined are responsible for the death of more than 150 million people, so how could that be true? Well, it is not true; it was stated to

Leadership Defined

(Email excerpt from Dr. Lee Thayer)

Leadership is as leadership does, of course.

But, just to gain a common perspective on this elusive concept, let us try this definition:

Leadership, from wherever it is exercised, has this universal characteristic: It changes the course of things...for the better IF worthy leadership, for the worse if not,

Whether that is changing the course of a conversation,

Or changing lives: yours first, then others, influencing how future lives will be lived, future perspectives altered,

The performance of an organization or a piece of an organization...

Of a gathering, a group, a community, a human endeavor (like music or marriage), or a whole society's trajectory.

In other words, it changes the course of history, writ small or large – the history of a life, a relationship, a vocational domain, a community, or an organization.

Without the intervention of competent leadership, things will simply evolve in the direction of the course they are on– teleologically. With worthy leadership, their trajectory is changed for the better, for all of those involved and thus for the larger social systems of which they are a part.

So, by this measure are you a leader?

provoke our thinking and inspire us to make a profound impact on the world as leaders—good leaders.

John Maxwell said, "Leadership comes down to this: influence." While Mao, Stalin, and Hitler certainly made their mark or, in Maxwell's words, had influence, something was missing in their modeling of leadership. Therefore, you must have more than influence to have an efficacious definition of leadership. This line of thought caused me to ponder deeply about what would be our organization's definition of leadership. What would be the anatomy to ensure we were singing from the same hymnal on "What is leadership?" The teleios (the purpose beyond the purpose of the definition) was a desire to ensure we dove deeper into thinking about The Anatomy of Leadership in order to improve our own leadership. Hence, The Anatomy of Leadership was born.

Dr. Thayer's thinking very much influenced the definition we came up with, and through the years, I have continued to add to this definition—the anatomy of "What Is This Thing Called Leadership?" I am paying it forward to you, the reader, to invite you on that same journey, which we will spend this book unpacking.

Epigraph

"In most cases, the leader of the future won't know enough to tell people what to do. The world is changing too rapidly. No one person will be smart enough to keep up. As Edgar Schein notes..., leaders will need to effectively involve others and elicit participation 'because tasks will be too complex and information too widely distributed for leaders to solve problems on their own."

Leader of the Future, The Drucker Foundation, 1996

"Conductors of great symphony orchestras do not play every musical instrument; yet through leadership the ultimate production is an expressive and unified combination of tones."

Thomas Bailey

"Everything rises and falls on leadership, everything."

John Maxwell

Introduction

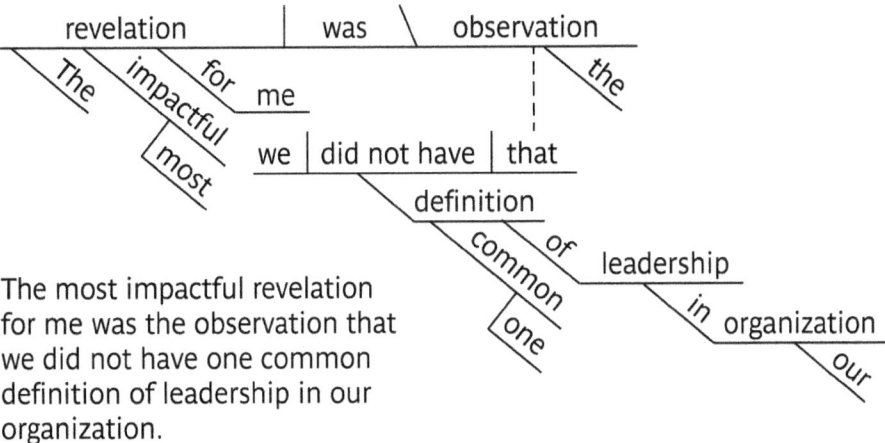

The most impactful revelation for me was the observation that we did not have one common definition of leadership in our organization.

Do you remember being in school and diagramming sentences? In a way, diagramming is dissecting the anatomy of a sentence. Years ago, my wife gave me a first edition of *The American Dictionary of the English Language* by Noah Webster, published in 1828. The dictionary defines anatomy as the art of separating the parts of an organism to ascertain their position, relations, structure, and function. In other words, something can be pulled apart and put into categories to better understand its gestalt. I remember one of my favorite teachers, Mrs. Wyble, demonstrating how diagramming parts of a sentence helps us achieve a deeper and better understanding of the whole.

The Anatomy of Leadership

I have spent most of my adult career in healthcare surrounded by caring, compassionate, and brilliant clinicians. I am constantly amazed by their talents and understanding of the complex universe of the human body. Clinicians must learn and understand years of research, dissection, and experimentation. The anatomy of the human body is a taxonomy, which means categorizing the groupings of systems of how the body works. These systems all work synergistically together, and just like diagramming sentences if you separate the pieces into categories, you will better understand the whole and how it all works together synergistically.

My aim with this book is to pull apart and categorize the vast and complex subject of leadership. I want to give you a framework to understand this broad subject so you can immerse yourself in your leadership journey and live your cause and purpose. I know this sounds bold, but hang with me, and you will see why I tie leadership with living your cause and purpose.

The book is divided into two sections. Part 1 of this book lays out The Anatomy of Leadership, the definition I have discovered through my reading and research. This includes categories with explanations to build a common lexicon of terms that will help you better understand the whole. In Part 2, we will unpack the 7 M's of the role of every leader;

Introduction

in other words, what you should be doing as you are on the journey to becoming a leader. Implementing the 7 M's will provide a path to better capacitate you to live your cause and purpose.

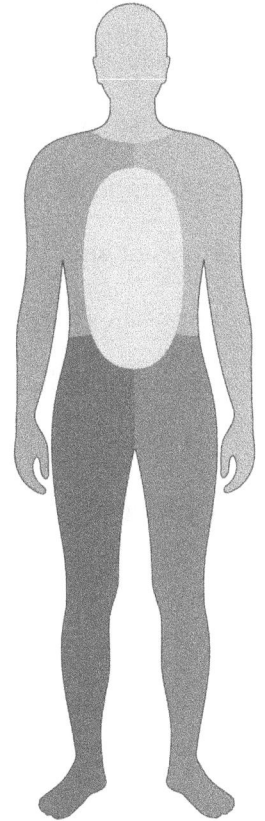

The Anatomy of Leadership Categories

This illustration is a metaphor utilizing human anatomy depicted vertically which will be filled in from Part I: Self-Mastery, Caring for Others, Influence, Intention, Cause and Purpose.

The 7 M's

This illustration is a metaphor utilizing human anatomy depicted horizontally and will be filled in from Part II: Mission, Margin, Meaning Management, Message into the Community, Making the Organization, Making People, and Mapping the Future.

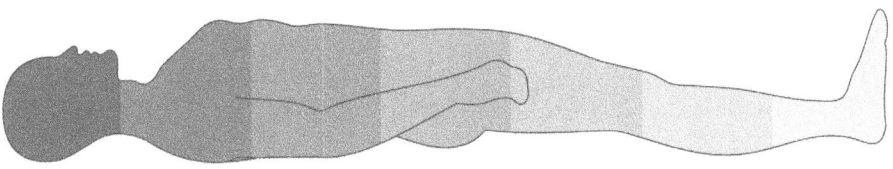

How to Use this Book/Workbook

I wrote this as a book and a workbook together. If you are like me, you own your books. What I mean by that is I write in them, dog-ear them, and try to learn from the book to change myself for the better. This book is organized to aid you, the reader, in both learning about leadership and interacting with the concepts in such a way that you can discover and live your cause and purpose with a toolbox of tools. With that bold purpose in mind, I have provided a workbook layout with plenty of journaling space. Therefore, own this book, mark all over it, and dog-ear it. I hope this book is of service to you on your leadership journey.

Use the space on the next page to take a few moments and jot down some thoughts before you jump into the rest of the book. Consider your reasons for reading this type of book. What do you hope to get out of it? Jot down your thoughts. It will be interesting to see at the end of this journey together if you got what you needed from this book and perhaps even more.

Introduction

So, let's jump in and unpack Part 1, The Anatomy of Leadership.

PART I
THE ANATOMY

"The virtue of all achievement is victory over oneself. Those who know this can never know defeat."

A. J. Cronin

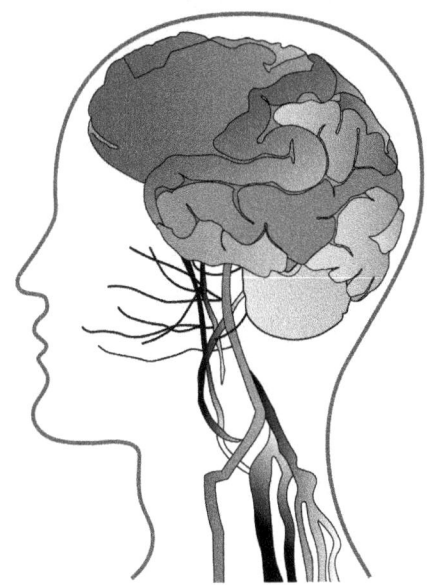

Chapter 1: *Self-Mastery*

- **Self-Mastery**
- Caring for Others
- Influence
- Intention
- Cause and Purpose

You cannot lead others if you are not on a journey to master yourself. The journey is lifelong with no specific destination, but you must be on it. What does that mean exactly? To effectively lead others, you must continuously strive to improve and become the best version of yourself.

I remember as a kid hearing King Solomon's story (1 Kings 3:3-15) and how God allowed him to ask for anything he wanted. He could have asked for riches, fame, fortune, etc. Can you imagine having that opportunity? What would you have asked for? Solomon asked for wisdom to be a good leader for God's people. God granted Solomon's wish and so much more. People came from all over the earth to hear his wisdom. That story inspired me at a young age, and I prayed for wisdom to be the best version of myself. Looking back almost fifty years into my life's journey, I know that while I am still a work in progress, I continue to learn and grow. As Robert Frost's poem "The Road Less Traveled" reminds us, "It has made all the difference." I want this for you, too. Self-mastery is the journey of becoming your best self.

"The Four Steps to Achievement - Plan purposefully. Prepare prayerfully. Proceed positively. Pursue persistently."

William Arthur Ward

Self-Mastery

All our life's journey moves us towards our cause and purpose, and leadership is the journey of living it. Taking the CEO role at Four Seasons in 2002 significantly accelerated my leadership journey. Prior to this, I was a CFO for a hospice in Pensacola, Florida. Before that, I worked for a Fortune 100 company, and before that, I worked for KPMG, one of the world's largest CPA and consulting firms. So while I had great business experience at a very young age, the Four Seasons CEO role was my toughest challenge to date. It was like *cresting one mountain range and seeing a new one rise before me*. A great nurse mentor taught me that analogy at Four Seasons. She would say, "You find yourself working so hard and putting all your energy and learning into cresting the mountain range in front of you. After much hard work and determination, you reach the top only to discover another mountain range looming before you. Such is the journey of life."

I am now close to thirty years of working in hospice and palliative care. As CEO of Teleios Collaborative Network (Teleios) and Teleios Consulting Group (Teleios), I do a lot of leadership coaching, training, speaking, and strategic planning. I have found that the mountain range analogy is comparable to our cause and purpose. We scale one mountain range with an early understanding of our cause and purpose only to get to another where a new level of understanding awaits us. In that spirit, my understanding of one of my purposes is to help other people find theirs, and the other is to help people live their purpose. I am convinced that living your purpose, whatever it is, comes down to leadership. What is leadership? It starts with self-mastery.

So, Where Should I Start?

Let's start with where you are today. Do you remember the old Clint Black song, "Wherever you go, there you are"? It's actually a great thought prodder. So today, are you where you wanted to be? And if you keep on this trajectory, will you be where you hope to be?

No one knows you better than you. Do you take time to self-reflect? Dr. Thayer taught us the term *de-center*, which means to step outside yourself. Another analogy I read about recently is to *go up on the balcony of your life*. What would you observe if you went up on a balcony and looked down on yourself?

- What strengths do you observe that need to be maximized and further honed?
- What are the opportunities for improvement you observe?

Self-Mastery

- Are you frivolous with your time?
- Are you too structured and unable to roll with the day's challenges?
- Are you too influenced by the opinions of others?
- Are you not influenced enough by the opinions of others?
- How focused are you with your time windows?

_____

_____

_____

_____

_____

_____

_____

_____

_____

Some Tools to Gain Self-Understanding

Many tools are available for self-assessment, which is a great place to start gaining self-understanding. At Teleios, we utilize *Management by Strengths* (MBS), a temperament assessment tool. While some might feel that temperament assessment is too narrow, it does help to bring self-awareness to each person's unique temperament. The model draws from the wisdom of Hippocrates, who observed that all humans have some combination of four basic temperaments:

- **Choleric (MBS Red)** - direct, action-oriented, and wired with an extreme sense of urgency.
- **Melancholy (MBS Yellow)** - very detailed oriented.
- **Phlegmatic (MBS Blue)** - harmonious and outwardly appear very laid back.
- **Sanguine (MBS Green)** - naturally outgoing and extroverted.

While MBS uses four basic colors to explain these temperaments, every person is a unique combination. MBS is an excellent tool to help you first understand yourself and then understand others. From there, you can learn, grow, and improve your communication and interaction skills, all of which contribute to self-mastery.

Self-Mastery

I discovered MBS through an interesting series of serendipitous circumstances. I once subscribed to John Maxwell's monthly leadership lessons. These came out on CDs, which tells you how long ago that was. On one of those monthly lessons, Maxwell said that the two most important books he had read were the Bible and *Personality Plus* by Florence Littauer. In *Personality Plus*, Littauer unpacks Hippocrates's four basic temperaments, which date to 400 B.C. One night, I was reading the book in bed, and my wife asked what I was reading. I explained that the supposition of the book is that there are four basic temperaments and that all people usually possess one primary and a secondary temperament. My wife said, "I don't think you can put people into boxes." I shared that I was reading the chapter on Melancholy. A trait of Melancholy temperaments is they do not believe you can put people in boxes. By the way, one of my wife's main temperaments is Melancholy. My wife said, "Give me that book."

While that comment irritated my wife, as usual, she was also correct. Understanding someone's temperament is not putting them in a box because, in reality, we are all a unique combination. It is as though when we were created, there were four glasses of temperament, and each of us received a unique mixture. The mixture is unique to us, yet it still comes from the four basic temperaments. Understanding these temperaments brings understanding about ourselves.

Another widely utilized tool that enables you to go deeper than MBS is *CliftonStrengths®*. The more you can fully grasp what makes you uniquely you, the better you can live your cause and purpose.

There is a shadow side to some of these tools. Some people fall into a rut in that they cite the tool to excuse certain habits or behaviors rather than using the tool for self-understanding to grow and improve. That is self-justification, not self-mastery. Be cautious not to slip into that mode of thinking when utilizing these tools.

I once worked on a project with a consulting organization and observed them using MBS. They utilized MBS for a season, but then people started to use their understanding of their temperament as an excuse. I am a Red, and used negatively, I can run over others. Rather it should have been used as, I have this self-understanding and embrace my temperament strengths while being mindful that each MBS temperament has a shadow side. I focus on learning and growing to ensure that I do not default myself, which means staying stuck in non-efficacious ways of being. Unfortunately, the consulting organization decided to quit using MBS, so they were throwing the proverbial baby out with the bath water.

Self-Mastery

All tools like MBS and *CliftonStrengths®* should help you understand how you were created and the unique toolbox of tools, gifts, and talents you have been given to hone, improve, and maximize to live your cause and purpose. These tools should also provide you with an understanding and awareness of where your growing edges are. However, here is the paradox. Some have bought into the lie that when they see mastery performed, they think, *Oh, they were just born that way.* No, they were born with the potential, but only through practice, learning, and self-mastery did those gifts become realized and maximized. Let me say that again. *The seed of mastery is within all of us; however, the road less traveled is for those who work at it and pay the price required for mastery to be realized.*

We are alive at a time when the best learning in the world is available at our fingertips. Through online tools like *Coursera*, you can take free classes from some of the greatest teachers in the world. All it takes is time and discipline. I implore you to work on mastering yourself. Many think of changing the world but forget that it starts with changing yourself. Realizing the best version of who you can be is an incredible journey, and much of what follows in this book builds upon this first part of *the anatomy of a leader.*

The Learning Mode

I have recently been reflecting on some of the greatest learning lessons from my time with Dr. Thayer, and probably *the most important one is the difference between the knowing mode and the learning mode.* The learning mode is a core necessity for the journey of self-mastery. What exactly are *the knowing mode* and *the learning mode?*

When I first heard Dr. Thayer use these phrases, I thought, *Surely I am in the learning mode, so let me check that box.* Not so fast, mister! The more time I spent around Dr. Thayer, the more I realized that most of my ideas and conversations were simply to prove my point. I realized this because his questions rattled my cage. I can still remember the day when, in one of his classes, I had a *Claritin commercial moment.* Like the commercial about "Claritin Clear," everything was in living color, and then a film was removed, and I could really see in living color. If you are of an older generation, think of black and white TV and the experience of seeing color TV for the first time. If you are a millennial or Gen Y, think of going from an HD TV to a 4K TV. The learning mode is like those analogies.

The journey from knowing mode to learning mode was difficult for me. The paradigm shift felt like my fingernails dragging across a chalkboard as my grip slipped away from the old as a new potential emerged. As the film was removed, I wondered why I had not lived like this before.

I began to engage in conversations and my day-to-day life like I had all the world to learn; therefore, I asked more questions. I would ask myself, *What is the best question to ask right now?* That simple shift began conversations like nothing I had experienced before. As Dr. Thayer said, "Questions are life-giving, statements, well…not so much."

Contrarily, the knowing mode is statement-oriented. The knowing mode is not inquisitive. It seeks to showcase what is already known rather than explore what could be missing. The knowing mode is bondage. It is also insidious and hard to shake.

Dr. Thayer often said, "Learning equals growth, and growth equals life." The learning mode is indeed life-giving, and it always starts with asking questions based on a general desire and curiosity to learn.

Let's try a thought experiment: Are you in the learning mode? How do you know? What did you learn yesterday? How did you learn it? Wrestle with those thoughts for a bit, then journal what comes to you.

My challenge to all of us, myself included, is to consistently pause and think, *What is the best question I can ask here?* Try this and see if it removes the film like the Claritin commercial and watch as your world begins to shift before your eyes.

_____

_____

_____

_____

_____

_____

_____

_____

_____

You Cannot Be Eclectic

A word of caution as there is a challenge to living in the information age and attempting to live life in the learning mode. Today, we have so many tools available to aid in self-improvement and self-mastery it can be overwhelming. At Teleios, we recommend that leaders develop learning plans for themselves. These specific care plans provide the basis for continuous improvement, enabling you to live your cause and purpose. Dr. Thayer used to say that knowing the difference between good advice and bad advice makes you a more discerning customer of what advice to take. This means you cannot be eclectic, flitting from one thing to another and thinking, *Oh, that is interesting! But that is interesting, too.* If a shiny, pretty, packaged book catches your fancy when you have no discernment of what you need at this stage of your journey, it will be hard to work on mastering yourself. You will flit from one project to another without ever really completing anything, akin to a home renovation project with hundreds of open tasks under some state of repair with no master plan for completion.

Years ago, I saw an interview with Jim Collins, the author of the book *Good to Great*. Collins relayed how one of his college professors profoundly impacted his life. He told him, "Jim, you need to work as hard at being *interested* as you work at being *interesting*." How many of us squander our time scrolling on social media to look for entertainment or to further our brand and gain followers? This trains our minds to be unfocused and without purpose, just flitting from one thing to another.

That habit then carries over into many areas of our life. It is much wiser to utilize our time with information that will improve us.

> **Cleaning House**
>
> My mom told me that when she and my dad were first married, she did not know how to keep a home. She would start vacuuming and then see a picture that needed hanging. She would quit vacuuming and begin hanging the picture, but while trying to get it straight, she would notice dishes in the sink. She would leave the picture and start washing dishes. Then, she would notice dust on the furniture. So she would leave the dishes and start dusting. By the end of the day, she had begun multiple tasks, but none were complete.
>
> My Cajun grandmother, in her wisdom, shared with my mom, "Sha (that's a Cajun term of endearment) you work hard, really hard, your mind works hard too. Perhaps you might be better served by making a list of all the tasks that need to be done. Then tackle the list one thing at a time until you complete everything." This great wisdom from my Cajun grandmother is very similar to the concept of a learning plan (a learning plan is like a renovation project task list but you are the renovation project) we will share at the end of this chapter.

Pushing Buttons

Have you ever heard the phrase *they push my buttons*? What exactly do we mean by that phrase? Have you ever stopped and considered your reactions to some people and, more importantly, some situations?

I had not considered this before, but in class one day, Dr. Thayer said, "Comeaux, do you know what I would do if I reported to you?" I thought, *Oh God, what a scary thought*. He went on to say, "I would do nothing but push your buttons." While Dr. Thayer was unusually skilled at rattling our cages, as he would call it, I always sensed he cared for us and wanted better for us. So I thought, *Surely, he is not just being mean or being a sadist*. So what was his point?

I began to keep a log throughout the week of situations and people where my buttons were pushed. You know those situations where you are literally hijacked, and it is like you are not in control of your faculties. It is like your emotions get the best of you.

I started to see interesting patterns, and I came up with a list of the top five situations that push my buttons.

Then I began to pray and journal about where those situations emerged in my life or, said another way, the parts of my story that were the headwaters. This exercise was incredibly enlightening, and I continue to work on these areas of my life even to this day because when your buttons are pushed, other people have control over you. When you are reacting to things, this is not leadership, and the more we grow in these areas, the more progress we are making on self-mastery.

Stop and consider: what situations push your buttons? Are there some themes? What is it about those situations that produce such reactions from you? Journal some thoughts.

_____

_____

_____

_____

_____

_____

_____

_____

_____

A Morning Routine

Throughout this book, I want to give you *tactics* as well as great *principles*, for one without the other is either theory with no application or application not rooted in any wisdom.

I have been on a journey of self-mastery for much of my life. One summer, when I was twelve, I spent a couple of weeks with my aunt. She said, "You are one of the most disciplined people I have ever met."

This was great affirmation at an early age. Some of this is my nature, but I was raised in a home where hard work was valued. We would wake up on Saturday mornings, and my dad would have a list of projects and chores for most weekends. The nurture of my upbringing also contributed to my discipline, but here is a key tip in case you say, "That's not me." The most impactful habit I have developed in the last fifty years has been a morning routine. Only in the last couple of years have I hardwired this, and the fruits have been exponential.

While I have been learning and growing most of my life, the joy of the journey has accelerated as I have adopted my morning routine. I have been on and off with morning quiet time and exercise for almost twenty years. However, for the past two years, my routine has been a 5 a.m. wake up, workout, quiet time, reading, and then I start my day. I have heard from master life coaches like Tony Robbins and Ed Mylett that if you create wins in the early morning hours, it impacts the rest of your day. I can now attest to that—*The 5 AM Club* by Robin Sharma is in the top five all-time books of my life. "Own your morning. Elevate your life" is a phrase used repeatedly in the book. And this one is my favorite, "Life's too short to play small with your talents." A morning routine can accelerate your journey towards self-mastery, and the fruits bestowed in every aspect of your life, including health, wealth, and well-being, are phenomenal.

> **"Your beliefs become your thoughts,**
> **Your thoughts become your words,**
> **Your words become your actions,**
> **Your actions become your habits,**
> **Your habits become your values,**
> **Your values become your destiny."**
>
> **Gandhi**

This brings us to the crux of this chapter: you can only accomplish what you are capable of accomplishing as a leader. The most important way to improve our leadership capacity is to master ourselves. To master ourselves means to master:

- Our emotions and our feelings
- Our thoughts
- Our words
- Our deliberate actions (or abstinence from them)

Before we fool ourselves into thinking that we can change others around us, let us remember the importance of first changing ourselves to what our cause and purpose require of us. This is the journey of self-mastery, the first part of The Anatomy of Leadership. Changing others is predicated upon what we learned in this chapter and is where we will focus next.

"Creators start at the end. First, they have an idea of what they want to create. Sometimes this idea is general, and sometimes it is specific. Before you can create what you want to create, you must know what you are after, what you want to bring into being."

Robert Fritz

Questions to Ponder

- What are your unique skills and talents?
- What understanding about yourself have you gleaned from tools like MBS or other self-assessment tools?
- What are your identified strengths? Have you maximized those? What are you doing to hone those further?
- What are your growing edges or the shadow side to your strengths? If you are unsure, do you have someone you know and trust to give you honest feedback?
- Do you have a learning plan? If not, what should be on your learning plan to improve yourself to be the type of leader others would want to follow? (see Appendix 1 Learning Plan template) Remember it is like a renovation project for yourself.
- Where would you like to see yourself in five years? At what level would you like to perform?
- Given your vision for five years from now, what skills do you need for that level of performance? What gaps do you have? How could you close those gaps?

Self-Mastery

"What this thing called leadership is all about: working within the organization to maximize the human potential inside of it."

Quint Studer

Chapter 2: *Caring for Others*

- **Self-Mastery**
- **Caring for Others**
- Influence
- Intention
- Cause and Purpose

At its basis, caring for others means that you will not let those with whom you have been entrusted to lead default themselves. You will provide guidance, challenge, mentorship, coaching, and unconditional love for them to realize their best selves. In other words, just as you have begun to help master yourself, you will help others by making it necessary that those around you become the best version of themselves as well.

Early Version of Caring for Others

I think the first time I began to live and understand this leadership principle was in high school. My two passions then were learning (I was a straight-A student and a bit of a geek) and football. My parents were paying a lot of money to send me to a Catholic school where many affluent families sent their kids. I did well and had all 100s in my classes (that is not an exaggeration), but I was not chosen for the National Honor Society. My parents were furious at this slight. A priest administrator told my mom, "Chris is a follower, not a leader." Upon reflection, this may have been an accurate statement at the time, but it is equally true that the school had an oppressive social hierarchy based on parental affluence. My parents pulled me out of this school and enrolled me in a different school with more blue-collar families.

Caring for Others

During my first football practice in spring training at the new school, I was recognized for my skill and my heart by many of the players. This recognition awakened something in me. They saw something in me I no longer saw in myself...potential. I ended up with so many great friends. We had a brotherhood, and I would do anything for those guys. We won a lot of games and had lots of adventures. However, during my senior year, my teammates wanted me to participate in a hazing ritual regarding some of the freshmen. I had endured similar treatment, and even worse, at the Catholic school. I did not feel it was the right thing to do, and I stood my ground. Many of the freshmen told me they appreciated this and sought my advice on other matters throughout the year.

Often, after football practice in the hot and humid Louisiana weather, I would run extra laps. At first, my teammates looked at me like I was crazy. However, by mid-season, several of them were running extra laps with me. Even some freshmen stuck around. I was not an incredibly talented football player. I had no great physical abilities, but worked hard, applied myself, and learned. Our team ended up going to the playoffs. Several of my teammates and I were chosen for honors, including playing in the state All-Star football game. What is my point? I loved those guys;

The Anatomy of Leadership

I even ended up with great relationships with some players from other teams. I wanted myself and all of them to dig deep and perform beyond what we thought possible. It was probably some of the beginning of my leadership journey and learning that if you genuinely care for others, they will find talents within themselves they perhaps did not know existed. It started with others seeing potential in me that rekindled a flame of belief in myself and my unique gifts. Then, I pushed myself hard, inspiring others to do the same. Leadership does that for you and it produces a beautiful multiplication effect on those around you.

What about you? Can you recall a time when you were part of a group, or someone saw something in you that you did not see in yourself? Journal about that.

_____

_____

_____

_____

_____

Caring for Others Defined

It is tough to lead a team if you are not on a journey towards self-mastery, which we now know means becoming the best version of yourself. When you are on this journey, you are in a much better position to challenge those you lead to also work on self-mastery. Not for the sake of performance but so these individuals can realize their true potential and find levels of performance within themselves they did not even know were possible.

Imagine a teacher, coach, team member, or leader who has brought out the best in you. Perhaps you just journaled about them. Did they pat you on the head and tell you, "You are wonderful!" Or did they challenge you by asking you tough questions? Were there times when you perceived they were being tough on you? And while they were challenging you, deep down inside, you sensed that they saw something in you that you knew was there but were unsure how to bring it out. Still, you trusted that, somehow, this is what they were after. *That is what caring for others looks like.*

Caring for others is not merely being demanding. Many people in the world demand from those they have been entrusted to lead, but the person being led usually senses that their leader does not have their best interests in mind. The leader who cares for others understands the person they are leading—their story and background and truly knows them. Often, a person who cares for us in this way can see things about us that we do not see in ourselves. They know the good, the bad, and the potential within us. The concept of de-centering (going up on the balcony of our life) referenced in the last chapter, is hard. To have someone who can give us an honest assessment from a vantage point of caring for us is invaluable to a person who genuinely wants to learn and grow.

Dr. Thayer used to say that all of humankind's behavior can be explained by this concept: people do what they do because *they can* and *they must*. Have you ever known someone to do something they seemed incapable of doing? With luck, they might pull it off once or twice, but consistency comes from competency. To care about others is to ensure they are preparing themselves to be the most competent person possible in their role, doing so because they can, based on their developed competency. For people to do something because they must, means that you as a leader possess the tool of making things necessary for those you lead. There is no Plan B. There is only Plan A, which is to learn and grow. If your team feels there are loopholes and inconsistencies, they will also sense you do not really care about them. If you are a permissive leader without standards, those around you will do all sorts of things but not the things needed for high performance.

During my morning routine, I usually listen to a podcast while working out. I love killing two birds with one stone. One of my team members at Teleios prefers the phrase *feeding multiple birds with one scone*. Use whatever analogy you like; my point is that if I can fold time upon itself and get multiple things done, then I am a happy man. Learning while working out is a two-for-one proposition. Recently, I was listening to the Huberman Lab podcast. Dr. Andrew Huberman is a very smart guy and said something that blew me away. He was interviewing Tony Hawk, the famous skateboarder. Apparently, Dr. Huberman was homeless as a teenager, and Tony's parents took him in. Usually, you do not put skateboarder and the word discipline together. However, Dr. Huberman said that Tony's dad had an enormous impact on his life because he was not scared to tell other kids what to do in sports and the skatepark. Dr. Huberman said, "I was at a time in my life where I had no discipline or direction." That is an example of caring for others, and it does not have to show up just at work; it can show up on the ballfield, at church, in the skateboard park, or in your community.

Caring for Others Applied

In my organization, Teleios, one of the first things we tell all new employees is that not hitting a deadline is unacceptable, but renegotiating it is. We call people on the carpet about this all the time. Why would we do that? Are we just trying to be nit-picky? No. We are making it necessary that our employees honor their word because integrity is one of our core values. Because we care about them and the type of person they are becoming, we hold them to a standard, demonstrating our care for them by example. We believe it even impacts what happens in their homes and personal relationships.

I once heard that John Wooden, the great basketball coach, demanded that his five-star athletes learn to tie their shoes as one of the first disciplines of playing for him. Why on earth would that matter? Because he knew that all world-class performance starts in the small things. Discipline in small things provides the scaffolding for a high-performance life. He cared enough about his players to ensure that the basics were in place, with nothing left to chance, so they could push the limits of their talents in ways that had never been seen on the basketball court. That is what leaders do—they make the right things necessary. This is the why behind the reason Dr. Thayer offered to push my buttons (i.e., the story I shared in Chapter 1). And that is what caring looks like.

> ## My Sixth Grade Teacher Made a Lifetime Impact by Caring for Others
>
> My sixth-grade teacher, Mrs. Wyble, modeled caring for others in such a way that she changed my life. I am sure if I canvassed any of my former sixth-grade classmates, they would say the same. The way she cared for others was brilliant. Do you know the poem "If" by Rudyard Kipling? To this day it is my favorite poem. For punishment, Mrs. Wyble would make us write the lines to "If" in lieu of standing in a corner and being paddled, which were favorite punishments of several other teachers. It was a Catholic school.
>
> Luckily, I did not have to write the poem many times, but when I did, I thought, *this is how I want to be when I grow up*. Even to this day, I read the poem at least once a year because it gives me a vision of what a person living a high-performance life should be like. Several years ago, that annual ritual inspired me to write my own poetry. This is funny because I am trained as an accountant, but I think Mrs. Wyble would be proud to know she made an indelible impact on me. Mrs. Wyble died during my sixth-grade year. Cancer took her, but she made a lifetime impact by caring for me and my fellow students. That is what caring for others does; it changes the trajectory of things, especially the lives of others you encounter.

"Leadership and learning are indispensable to each other."

John F. Kennedy

Not That Type of Caring

I have spent most of my career in the field of hospice, which is a very caring and compassionate environment. Translating this type of caring and compassion by the bedside produces some of the most amazing healthcare and lifecare seen anywhere. On the flip side, hospice leaders often interpret caring for their staff to mean:

- Coddle your staff
- Do not upset them
- Make them happy
- Pat them on the back
- Be nice to them

The bullets above are not the recipe to help someone find new frontiers of who they can become, nor do they build a platform for organizational success. Rather, leading others with the above as the only tools in your toolbox will breed sloppiness, complacency, and an entitlement mentality, and it will show up by the bedside as non-excellent care.

Hospice and palliative care work is hard and taxes the emotional reserves, unlike other healthcare work. Grief is real. Leaders in this field must be aware and competent in this area and must also couple that competence with making the right things necessary. Interestingly, due to the COVID-19 pandemic, mental and emotional health understanding and proficiency are now essential skills of all leaders, according to one of my other mentors, Quint Studer. I had the privilege of working with Quint at his company, Studer Group. I often refer to my time at Studer Group as my time in the business equivalent of the *Navy Seals* because that is what it felt like to me. I have never worked harder and learned more than in my time there. I have been blessed with great mentors, and Quint is one of these. He is a leader that demands much. Deep down, I knew it was because he cared for me and wanted the best out of me and for me. I recently was able to host Quint on my podcast *TCN Talks*. Many of us have heard the term, soft skills, which refers to things like emotional intelligence, mental health, and self-awareness. On this podcast, Quint called mental and emotional health skills and tools *essential skills*. He nailed something I had thought for a long time but did not have the lexicon to pay it forward. Quint is right, and in many respects, mental and emotional health understanding and proficiency have always been essential for hospice leaders, but now they are necessary and essential for all leaders. The challenges have always been there, but the COVID-19 pandemic created a challenge unlike anything we had seen before in healthcare and surfaced a requirement that has always been needed.

For you and me, caring for others you have been entrusted to lead means that you are working as hard on mastering yourself as you are making it necessary for those you lead to do the same. If you merely did those two things, you would be better for it, and your team would be better for it, but to what end? We will go there next in the next chapter of *The Anatomy of Leadership*.

"You cannot give what you do not have, and self-improvement precedes team improvement. Here's what I know – the only way that I can keep leading is to keep growing. The day that I stop growing, somebody else takes the leadership baton. That's the way it always is."

John Maxwell

Questions to Ponder

- How do you interpret caring for others now?
- Has your current definition been helpful to you and your current team or past teams? How would you know? What fruits or results do you have?
- Can you think of a teacher or coach in the past who you felt was hard on you but that you knew cared for you and made you want to work even harder for them? How does your style emulate some of what that person did for you?
- Given this chapter, are there some areas you need to work on and add to your learning plan to help you better care for those you have been entrusted to lead?
- Have you been given leadership over some domains? Are you caring for your folks in these domains? What would they say?

_____

_____

_____

_____

The Anatomy of Leadership

"Proactive people...work on the things they can do something about. The nature of their energy is positive, enlarging, and magnifying, causing their Circle of Influence to increase."

Stephen Covey

Chapter 3: *Influence*

- **Self-Mastery**
- **Caring for Others**
- **Influence**
- Intention
- Cause and Purpose

John Maxwell summed up all of leadership with this one word: influence. What does influence mean? According to the *Merriam-Webster Dictionary*, influence is *the act or power of producing an effect without apparent exertion of force or direct exercise of command.*

You could say influence is the weight of who you are as a leader. Stephen Covey calls it your *circle of influence*. He would explain it this way, "You can put all things that happen to you in life on one of two walls, that which you can influence and the other which are things outside your control." Covey advised us to, "Let those outside our control go and focus on that which we can influence." In other words, focus your time, attention, and energy in your circle of influence.

Focusing on your circle of influence is a great exercise because too many people put their energy, effort, and focus into areas outside their influence, especially in today's hyper-charged, social media-addicted world.

Covey went on to further expound on this concept by using three circles:

- **The circle of concern** is a wide range of concerns we might have about a topic. Don't worry about this stuff. Notice the lexicon of concern rather than worry.

Influence

- **The circle of influence** narrows the first circle into those concerns we can do something about—directly or indirectly. Leadership resides in this circle and the circle of control.
- **The circle of control** is the area that we have control over.

Covey tells us that our circle of influence is often smaller than the circle of concern in life. For example, we can't control the economy or a company merger. As we react, we tend to focus on the circle of concern, which depletes our energy because we have no control over it. Leaders put their focus in their circle of influence and in their circle of control.

What are in your circles of influence and control? Only areas you can directly influence or control should be in that circle. Toward what specific things should you give your time and energy?

_____

_____

_____

_____

_____

_____

The paradox of life is that as you put your energy and focus on what should be in your circle of influence and your circle of control, the weight of who you are grows. When you make an impact in your circle of influence and control, your circles grow and enlarge. Through my fifty-plus years on this earth, I have found that my circles of influence and control have grown to include things I used to identify as outside my circle. This is the benefit of focusing on your circles of influence and control. Unfortunately, today's culture sells a seductive lie—getting us to focus on almost everything outside of our circles, which causes us to be minimally impactful.

Light diffused gives light to a small room. Light diffused in a large space barely brings any illumination, but focused light like a laser beam can cut through a steel I-beam. Therein lies *the secret of influence: it is all about where you put your focus.*

"Your calling should be your territory."

Sunday Adelaja

Influence

A Great Example of Working in Your Circle of Influence

Jean Moulthrop Hoogstra was the matriarch of Four Seasons Hospice. She is a splendid example of someone using their circle of influence. Mrs. Jean, as I called her, buried four husbands during her life. She married her last husband, Don, at eighty-five and would often say he was the love of her life.

When Mrs. Jean's first husband passed away, he left Mrs. Jean and a two-year-old daughter with a mortgage and no visible means to support themselves. Her husband was a salesman, so Mrs. Jean took over his sales territory. Within one year, she became the top salesperson in Michigan.

Later in life, Miss Jean moved to Hendersonville, North Carolina. In her living room, over soup and sandwiches, she helped found what later became Four Seasons Hospice, where I have spent a large portion of my professional career. This was at a time when Elisabeth Kübler-Ross inspired many to challenge the prevailing healthcare industry that death and dying was not done well in our country. This was on the heels of a revolution in the birthing movement, and it was only natural to see questions on the other end of the continuum of life. Mrs. Jean was a pioneer. She recognized that her community needed a hospice. Little did she know how far what she started would go and how its influence would grow.

The Anatomy of Leadership

During my tenure as CEO of Four Seasons, we often honored Mrs. Jean because the organization and the tens of thousands of people we had the privilege to care for would not have existed except for her circle of influence. We conducted the largest capital campaign in Henderson County history to construct the Greatrex Administrative Building and expanded Four Seasons' Hospice House, the Elizabeth House. At the ribbon-cutting ceremony, Mrs. Jean was overwhelmed to see how far the organization she had helped found in her living room had come. That is the beauty of working in your circle of influence; it can grow beyond your comprehension.

The metaphor Quint Studer used at the Studer Group to illustrate the impact one could make on the world was the concentric rings that fan out when you drop a pebble in a pond. I think that is right on point because as you focus on your circle of influence, it grows bigger and bigger.

A few years before she passed away, Mrs. Jean shared with me the story of the maintenance person at the continuing care retirement community where she lived. She said people would make up service calls just to have this gentleman visit with the retirees in the community. He was an incredible person who used the platform of a maintenance position to be the sunshine of many elderly people's day. He died unexpectedly from a heart attack, and more than a thousand people attended his funeral. His life teaches a great lesson: it does not matter what circle of influence or domain you have been given; the question is, what will you do with it?

What circles of influence have you been given domain over?

_____

_____

_____

_____

_____

_____

_____

My Own Example

At the age of twenty-five, I became Chief Financial Officer of a hospice in Pensacola, Florida. I did not know much about leadership, but I was eager to learn, and Stephen Covey's *7 Habits of Highly Effective People* profoundly impacted me. I focused on my circle of influence, so much so that it led me to my next job as the CEO at Four Seasons in Asheville, North Carolina, at the age of thirty.

I received that opportunity because a friend was visiting our hospice in Pensacola to perform an audit. Our team had been working for a couple of years to ensure that our back-office areas, which were my responsibility, were performing with a high level of customer service. We even had a mission statement just for our departments that said, "Superior Customer Service in All That We Do." It was so simple, yet so profound. Our departments did not directly care for patients; however, we wanted to remind ourselves that our work could impact those caring for patients simply by how we treated them. Certainly, there were days we fell short, but that ideal called us forward. It enabled us to use our influence. My friend was on the board of the Four Seasons Hospice in North Carolina. He was so impressed by what he saw in Pensacola that he asked me to interview for the CEO role at Four Seasons. I was selected for the role in 2002. This forever shaped my life and my family's life and continues to hold a special place in my heart. In fact, the community of Hendersonville, North Carolina, where Four Seasons is based, is still where I call home and where my wife and I have raised our five children.

I use this example to demonstrate how utilizing your circle of influence and focusing on those you have been entrusted to lead will grow your circle over time, especially if you are intentional about the focus of your influence. If every leader utilized their circle of influence for good at home and work, the world would certainly be a better place.

Think about the circles you have been given domain over and your tenure in those circles. Now, look in the rearview mirror. Are those circles better with you as a part of them? How so? Journal about it.

_____

_____

_____

_____

_____

_____

_____

It starts with what is in front of you right now. What is in your circle of influence? Is it a team, a department, an organization, a little league team, or a Sunday school class? Whatever it is, make that circle better than you found it. Be on the journey of self-mastery. Care for those in your circle well, and you will see your circle grow.

"My mission is to be a positive, uplifting, constructive, and healing influence in the lives of those I touch."

Laurie Buchanan, PhD

You can only see your circle grow if you are intentional; that is what we will explore next.

Questions to Ponder

- How does your daily performance of your role affect others? Is it for the good or for the bad?
- What and/or who is in your circle(s) of influence?
- How focused are you on your circle of influence? Do you find yourself diffused over too many areas that really are not part of your

Influence

role or circle of influence today? Do you need to step out of some of these areas?

- Who is someone you admire for their leadership? How do you see them utilizing the circle of influence they have been given?
- How are you using your influence?
- What challenges or barriers have you tolerated to preclude you from making the most of the circle of influence you have?
- Does anything need to be added to your learning plan from this chapter?

_____

_____

_____

_____

_____

_____

_____

_____

The Anatomy of Leadership

"We gain confidence when we know who we are, what makes us significant, and the essence of our true value."

Chip Madera

Chapter 4: *Intention*

- **Self-Mastery**
- **Caring for Others**
- **Influence**
- **Intention**
- Cause and Purpose

You must be intentional to be a leader. You are not a leader if you react to things rather than being proactive. A leader changes things for the better. Are you aware of your presence and energy? Are you intentional with them? Do you react to events or act upon them to change their trajectory?

Journal your thoughts on these questions.

_____

_____

_____

_____

_____

_____

Years ago, when I worked for Quint Studer at the Studer Group, I got to shadow some amazing leadership coaches as part of my orientation. We did an assessment of a hospital in California. It was one of the most challenging environments I have witnessed to date. Walking into the hospital, it felt like darkness and apathy were palpable. I participated in a tour early in the day, and something stood out. One nurse on the surgical ward literally radiated light. If you have seen

Intention

the *Lord of the Rings* scene where Gandalf lit his staff in the cave and said, "You shall not pass," it symbolizes what was emanating from this remarkable woman. Her presence stood out dramatically in contrast to the rest of the hospital and staff.

We conducted focus groups throughout the day; she was in my last group. I had the opportunity to share with her my experience of walking through the hospital and witnessing how she stood out. She teared up and shared something with me that I will never forget.

She said, "Yes, this hospital is a dark place to work. There are cultural issues, leadership issues, resource issues, tough patient issues, and on and on it goes. But years ago, when I worked for another hospital, I was sent to the Disney Institute's healthcare experience, and the one thing I remember was the concept of being *on stage* and *off stage*."

She said she carried the idea with her each day and chose the attitude and spirit she would reflect. She realized her attitude and presence would emanate no matter the external circumstances and challenges. She solidified the importance and possibility of being intentional regardless of the circumstances she would find herself in. This incredible nurse was so intentional about her presence. When she was at her nurse's station, she knew she was on stage. In the break room or locker room, she might break down and cry due to workplace challenges, but when on stage, she made the choice to be intentional because she knew that intention would impact others. For me, this became such a powerful testimonial of the power of intention.

Shakespeare said, "All the world's a stage." What does that mean in the context of intention? It means we all can approach life as an on-stage and off-stage proposition. If you have a meeting on Zoom, how are you showing up? Are you intentional? What about a one-to-one meeting with your staff? How intentional are you? What about when you walk through your organization? How intentional are you? Replay the movie in your mind of some of those interactions over the last couple of weeks. How intentional were you? Were you acting upon things or reacting to them? Journal your self-assessment.

_____

_____

_____

_____

_____

Intention

Energy Aids Intention

In many hospices we work with via Teleios, we utilize Jon Gordon's book *The Energy Bus*. Gordon illustrates the power of intention regarding the energy we choose and our impact on every facet of our lives by being intentional with our energy. There is even a whole industry emerging about how to cultivate more energy, bring more energy, and project energy. All that thought is predicated upon the idea that you have a choice; you can be intentional on a day-to-day basis. Do you believe this?

Years ago, I was walking through our inpatient unit observing operations after a patient complaint resulted in a visit from state surveyors. We had been having some leadership challenges in the facility, so I knew our staff in the unit was fragile. At the same time, we had been through several challenging patient and family situations with clinically complex occurrences. I intentionally walked over to interact with staff while the surveyors conducted their complaint survey. I knew I needed to carry myself with a spirit that would convey confidence. I visited the nursing station where many staff members were positioned and asked one of the key influencers on shift how she was doing. Understandably, she said she was nervous due to the survey. I could sense the fear and nervousness, and I could sense the same from all the nurses at the station. I looked the nurse in the eye and then faced the rest of the team. They all seemed to turn to me at the same moment. With a look of trust in them and confidence in our team, I simply said, "You guys got this." It was not the most rousing or memorable speech, but years afterward, staff recounted that moment back to me and what it meant to them. It shows the power of intention. The survey ended with no substantiated findings, and the team gained confidence in themselves that they carried forward. Years later, team members still tell me how my words impacted them. It is amazing that such a tiny act would be remembered, but such is the value of playing your role with intention.

It matters how you are performing your role. Are you reacting to things or being intentional? Are you aware of the energy you are projecting? What is its impact on others?

Intention

"Intention becomes reality."

Janet Bull, MD and retired Chief Medical Officer of Four Seasons

The Tone You Set

I have read several *Harvard Business Review* articles that I consider *best of the best*, including an article I read during my first year as a leader in 1995. The gist of the article was this: The spirit you carry yourself with will pervade your team. Here is the kicker: this is true even if you do not interact with them. You can shut the door of your office, and your attitude and spirit will pervade whether you intend it to or not. This is why choosing intentionality is so important. Our intentionality can and will impact others around us. The opposite is also true. If you are not intentional and are harboring negativity, even if you think you are keeping it to yourself, that spirit can pervade your team. Intentionality can set the tone in a team, an organization, or even a family.

Here is a funny example that stuck with me from home:

My third son's name, Declan, means *man of prayer*. One night, his brother said grace for our meal, and when he finished, Declan looked at him and said, "That was a damn good prayer!"

He was four at the time, and as much as I wanted to correct him about his language, it struck me that I knew where he got that language—

> ### The Tone at the Top
>
> When I was a young auditor in my first job out of college, I had a great mentor and managing partner I worked with at KPMG. Something he said to me struck me as very profound, "You can sit in a room verifying numbers all day, and it will not tell you anything about the business, but you can spend one hour with the CEO or the senior team, and it will illuminate what you see in the numbers."
>
> He called it *the tone at the top*. I have seen that lesson demonstrated within most of the organizations I have coached and spent time with, and I have even seen this in play at home and in my own organization.
>
> What exactly is the tone at the top? Simply put, it is the tone the CEO and senior team intentionally and unintentionally set. Said another way, the spirit they carry blended like some mixed drink produces a tone at the top that seeps down into the organization.

Intention

my tone at the top influenced him when I was not intentional about my words and influence.

I have seen both good and bad examples of the tone on top.

The Good:

- Leaders are affirming and encouraging, and that example cascades down throughout the organization.
- Truth telling is modeled and permeates all communication.
- Service is highly esteemed, and the organization models excellent service.

The Bad:

- Accountability is not valued and produces a very inconsistent culture where follow through is not exhibited.
- Harmony is valued above all else, and the shadow side is a lack of urgency and an inability to have tough conversations and create accountability.

These examples beg the question for all of us: What is our tone at the top? Take an inventory of the positives, and the unintentional tones that may be influencing your organization through your spirit as a leader.

_____

_____

_____

_____

_____

_____

If you have a trusted advisor, it is wise to ask them these questions. Often, they can see more clearly as they are not as close to the situation and will not share the same emotions about your leadership style and tone as you do. Coaching from them can help you turn the mirror to see how your tone at the top creates the culture around you.

So how about you? How intentional are you each day with your energy and the spirit you evoke? What tone do you think you set for your team, organization, or even your family?

Some Tools to Help

Intentionality in attitude, presence, energy, and confidence comes from being prepared. There are several tools in the Teleios Leadership

Intention

System that we teach to give confidence to leaders. The confidence you gain in having a plan enables you to be more intentional each day and helps you be better prepared to act upon things rather than reacting. A few such tools we teach are:

- **Weekly Big Rocks –** This is a weekly exercise based on the principle I saw Stephen Covey teach years ago. He had three buckets separately filled with big rocks, gravel, and sand. He would ask a volunteer to put everything in one bucket. If you have never seen the video, watching the volunteer try to push the big rocks into the sand is always entertaining. It never works. You must put the Big Rocks in first, then the gravel, and lastly the sand; then everything miraculously fits. *The learning lesson is to identify your Big Rocks first.* At Teleios, we use this lexicon in our weekly and daily reviews as we prepare our task list so we know the most important things we need to get done each day.

  It is almost paradoxical in its application. By its very nature, identifying your Big Rocks and committing to focusing on them is leadership in action—intentionally acting upon the world rather than merely reacting to the world or what others dictate to you is leadership.

- **Role Description** – So what is a role description? It outlines the contributions required of the role for the organization to fulfill its cause and purpose in the future. Every person performs a role even when they are unaware they are performing. As we said earlier, Shakespeare said, "All the world is a stage." Some think this means being fake, but whether you realize it or not, you are performing something. The question is, are you performing what needs to be performed in the moment, and are you performing it intentionally? Most people perform their roles in default settings, which means they default themselves. It is not intention, nor is it chosen based on what is required. Instead, the habits and results of years past dictate how someone shows up. They perform whatever their habit is, even if that is what is not needed in the moment and in a specific situation. A role description can help paint the picture of what role needs to be performed to help your organization, team, family, or other group achieve its intended destiny. Roles either contribute positively or negatively to the outcomes of the organization.

    A role description can be powerful. In *The 7 Habits*, Stephen Covey says you are your own computer programmer. You write the script and then live it. Dr. Thayer was Covey's mentor, so it is the

Intention

same principle, just a different way of teaching. So here are some questions to consider in composing your role description. What am I at this organization for? Why do I exist? What is my purpose in life? What do I dream of accomplishing in life? What is the ideal in my role? How can I live with purpose and joy in all my roles in life? Contemplate those questions and then take a stab at your role description below. If helpful, we have included my full role description in Appendix 2.

_____

_____

_____

_____

_____

_____

_____

_____

Regardless of the circumstances, these tools, while not panaceas or silver bullets, help build the muscle of being intentionally prepared. Preparation promotes adaptability and improvisation in leadership, which enable intentionality.

Intentionally Performing My Role

When I was in Dr. Thayer's Master in Leadership program, he challenged us to learn how a well-crafted role description requires you to *perform your role regardless of the circumstances*. During this time, the team I worked with launched a radio program to build the brand of our hospice. The radio program was titled *Healthcare Café*, and I really enjoyed doing the shows. However, during one week, I was sick with a chest cold. I am not sick very often, and very rarely am I sick enough to stay home from work and stay in bed, but this was a time when most people would have. As I decided what to do, I remembered my role description and the key phrase, *regardless of the circumstances*. I dug deep and thought, *what an incredible challenge*.

Live programs like radio are challenging because you need to know your subject, think on your feet, and still make it entertaining—a challenge on your best day, much less when you feel horrible. I gave that

Intention

program my all that day, and it turned out incredible. I was intentional and performed my role regardless of the challenge (note that I was fully isolated and alone in the recording booth, so I did not infect anyone else during the show's taping of the show). In full disclosure, I did go home right after and slept the rest of the day. But I can share with you that something shifted in me that day. It built a deeper confidence, and my intentionality muscle grew. I am not saying the learning lesson is working sick because caring for our health is important. But on that particular day, it was something I was supposed to do. It was keeping a commitment to myself and others.

I have a few other examples. During the COVID-19 pandemic, when I did not travel on a committed trip, I did the opposite. I can see in the rearview mirror that those were also the right decisions. However, on that day, envisioning the role that I needed to perform, and performing it regardless of the circumstances, has been a source of strength I pull from even still. One of the examples I can point to is that I now host one of the top-rated podcasts in the hospice and palliative care space called *TCN Talks*. As I prepare for each show, I still remember that radio program. I think that *if I could bring my "A" game on that day, I can do even better today*. The value of being intentional echoes throughout our lives, propelling us to better live our cause and purpose. I am living proof.

"By centering our lives on timeless, unchanging principles, we create a fundamental paradigm of effective living. It is the center that puts all other centers in perspective."

Stephen Covey

Questions to Ponder

- How intentional are you as a leader regarding your presence?
- What energy are you projecting on a daily basis? How do you know?
- When going into a meeting, do you consider that you are walking onto a stage to perform your role? This is a good place to consult your role description or to create one.
- Think about the concept of being on stage and off stage. How intentional are you when you are going on stage? You are performing whether you know it or not. How impactful is your performance?
- Do you give yourself permission to be unintentional based on how you are feeling? Are you too impacted by the cross-currents of emotion? In other words, do you allow the ups and downs of your

Intention

feelings to dictate how you show up? What tone does that set with your team? What fruits does that produce with your team?

- What part do you play in the feelings and emotions of your team? Do you find the more intentional you are, the tone you set has a more positive impact on you and your team?

_____

_____

_____

_____

_____

_____

_____

_____

_____

"This is the true joy in life: being used for a purpose recognized by yourself as a mighty one; being a force of nature instead of a feverish, selfish little clod of ailments and grievances complaining that the world will not devote itself to making you happy. I am of the opinion that my life belongs to the whole community, and as long as I live it is my privilege to do for it whatever I can. I want to be thoroughly used up when I die, for the harder I work the more I live. I rejoice in life for its own sake. Life is no 'brief candle' for me. It is a sort of splendid torch which I have got hold of for the moment, and I want to make it burn as brightly as possible before handing it on to future generations."

- George Bernard Shaw

Chapter 5: *Cause and Purpose*

- **Self-Mastery**
- **Caring for Others**
- **Influence**
- **Intention**
- **Cause and Purpose**

The Anatomy of Leadership

The last segment of The Anatomy of Leadership is a great cause and purpose. I remember contemplating Dr. Thayer's challenge regarding who were the great leaders of the 20th Century, and it occurred to me that Mao, Stalin, and Hitler were working on some version of Self-Mastery. They challenged others, although I would say they were weak on that point. However, they did push others to achieve levels beyond expectations. Mao, Stalin, and Hitler certainly had influence and were intentional in much of what they did. So, what was missing? They were missing a great cause and purpose that made the world a better place.

A great cause and purpose will fuel you on the bad days and give you focus on all days. Cause and purpose are your *why*, and if that *why* helps others and harmonizes with their own whys, then you are on to something.

What is your cause and purpose? I know this is a tough question. I have wrestled with it most of my life. When we hear such a question, we may envision the skies parting and a tablet descending from on high containing your special assignment, like an episode of *Heavenly Mission Impossible*.

In my experience, at different stages of your life, your cause and purpose are unveiled to you little by little. Like the mountain range

Cause and Purpose

analogy in Chapter 1, you crest one range to find another before you. In other words, unveiling your cause and purpose happens through life's journey and getting quiet with a journal and pen. You ask the question and attempt to put what comes to mind into words. Repeat this exercise on an annual basis. By revisiting what I have previously written, I have found that my grasp of my cause and purpose is increasingly clear. Like looking through a telescope at the moon, it is at first blurry, but then, as you dial in, it becomes clearer and clearer. At the same time, you are glancing back through the rearview mirror of life, making sense of what has transpired. Our cause and purpose will not come with immediate clarity but rather with increasing clarity as we dial in over time. In essence, what is most important is to wrestle and keep wrestling at intervals in life with the question: What is my cause and purpose?

He who knows the "why" for his existence, he will be able to bear almost any "how."

Viktor Frankel

Here are some challenges that may arise as you wrestle with cause and purpose:

What if my current job does not align with what I think is my cause and purpose? This is a question I have asked over the years. In fact, I once sought wisdom from Dr. Thayer, as my role at the time was not a perfect fit with my emerging understanding of my cause and purpose. Two major job opportunities came my way, and I was wrestling with which path to take. Should I stay where I was, or did one of these new opportunities align more with my cause and purpose? When I asked Dr. Thayer which I should choose, his response astounded me. He said, "I don't know, but I think you should pick one and go to school there because the discipline will do you good."

Over the years, I have unpacked so many rich lessons from that simple statement. Still, the biggest one I pay forward to you is this: Wherever you are, even if you choose only to be in your role for thirty more days, *go to school there*, which means be a sponge, learn all you can, and apply yourself with 100% effort. The discipline and the learning will do you good. I have found that this gives you greater clarity about your cause and purpose. Also, what you learn provides tools that will be helpful later, even if it doesn't seem so at the time.

Cause and Purpose

A tougher question is, can you really find a job that perfectly aligns with your cause and purpose? It is nearly impossible to nail this in your first job because it is through living and learning that you gain better clarity on your cause and purpose. It involves *going to school* wherever you are, becoming more discerning, and better aligning your role with your cause and purpose. The more I have done this, the more I feel that I do not have a job but rather that I love what I do. The quote, "For this is why I have come, for this is me," has become truer and truer to me. Epictetus, the Greek philosopher, struck upon this wisdom as well. He said, "Although we cannot control which roles are assigned to us, it must be our business to act our given role as best we can and to refrain from complaining about it. Wherever you find yourself and in whatever circumstances, give an impeccable performance." There are so many examples in my own life where this has been true.

"Catch a revelation of who you are and change will be nothing."

Patrick Waters

The Anatomy of Leadership

In *Positive Intelligence,* author Shirzad Chamine emphasizes that finding your cause and purpose is as much about the journey as the destination. Shirzad says, "Many people think that the answer to the meaning of life will one day emerge with fanfare and fireworks. They feel stuck because they don't have full clarity about their purpose in life or what would make their life happiest or most meaningful. I tell them to consult their Sage's Navigation compass for their little steps, knowing that these steps will eventually get them to a very meaningful place."

Without a sense of your cause and purpose, it is hard for a person to be a leader. You could harness all the other aspects of the anatomy and definition of being a leader, but without this one, you will be a shadow of the leader you could be otherwise.

When I look in the rear-view mirror of my leadership journey, I want to apologize for how I led in the past. Some of my friends and co-workers from my past might be surprised for me to write that, as I still have relationships and contact with many whom I had the privilege of leading back in my mid-twenties. Usually, they are very complimentary of our time together. But being on the learning journey, if I knew back then what I have learned throughout, I can see how I could have been more impactful for each of the team members I had the honor and privilege

Cost Accounting

In college, one of the classes I hated was cost accounting. Truth be told, I would pull all-nighters and cram before a test. It was a binge and purge cycle because, after the test, I did not retain much. I did get an A in the class, barely.

My second job out of college was an incredible opportunity. It was an executive development program where I traveled worldwide auditing the operations of, wait for it…a manufacturing organization. This meant I needed great competence in cost accounting. This job was the only time in my life that I was put on a performance action plan, specifically because I did not have the necessary knowledge in cost accounting. So, what did I do? I pulled out my college textbook and studied every night and every weekend.

By the time I finished the two-year rotation of international travel, my leader said, "We are not sure what we are going to do without Chris in this program. He is the anchor and has become the mentor to many on the team." They even had me teaching some of the other team members cost accounting. In my next job as a CFO for a hospice, my knowledge of cost accounting helped me think creatively regarding healthcare finances, unlike any of my peers.

The moral of the story is if you *go to school* wherever you are, even if it does not feel like something you love or want to do the rest of your life, it will pay dividends. For me, it led to eventually getting my first CEO position with Four Seasons Hospice, which absolutely has been critical to discovering my cause and purpose. It all has worked together for good, but I would have missed it and could still be in the wilderness if I had not applied myself and gone to school there during challenging stretches. What I learned during these times has helped clarify my cause and purpose.

of leading. Being clear on your cause and purpose and leading from that place enables you to more significantly impact your circle of influence and the people in that circle. I can see that in my rearview mirror. My point is not to live with regret; my point is I can see upon reflection that *I am more impactful as a leader the more I understand my cause and purpose.*

Your cause and purpose are as much about the people you have been entrusted to lead as it is about you. Living your cause and purpose impacts those around you, and in turn, as they live their cause and purpose, this impacts those around them. Ultimately, whatever your organization does will impact the customers your organization is serving. The many projects you work on to make those things happen are just circles of influence for cause and purpose to be played out. Cause and purpose are a force multiplier for all the other aspects of The Anatomy of Leadership that we have discussed thus far.

What We Think We Become

What role does thinking play in our cause and purpose? Thinking is a double-edged sword. Recently, at church, a video was shown of a man going through life while the audio verbalized what was playing through his head: a cacophony of thoughts continuously playing while the man

Cause and Purpose

monotonously woke up, got ready for work, drove to work in his BMW, worked in a cubicle at his job, drove back home, sat on his couch and watched TV, and then woke up and did it all over again.

The paradox was that the man in the video was supposedly living the American dream, quite like many of us. But stepping back from the thoughts in his head, he was a rat in a maze dictated purely by his habits. He was dancing to someone else's tune. While living the American dream with the BMW, the nice job, and the nice house, he was indeed thinking, but was he thinking about the right things? His thoughts informed his habits, his habits formed his routine, and his routine was his life.

This illustration is indicative of many people today. We are running fast to catch the American dream, but in reality, we are running nowhere, and our thoughts play a major role in that destination. Most people do not have a cause or a real purpose for being. Even if someone knows their cause and purpose, they may not intentionally form their thoughts around it or realize the power that those thoughts hold over their ultimate destination.

2 Corinthians 10:5 instructs us to "take every thought captive," a statement which, by its very nature, indicates that we have the power to control and direct our thoughts with intentionality.

More than ever before, living in this high-tech, breakneck-pace time necessitates knowing our cause and purpose, being disciplined in our thinking, and centering our thoughts upon that cause.

High intention for your cause will help you weld, mold, and shape your habits. High intention in thought, high intention in asking questions of the world, and high intention in action—that is what is required of us to identify and live our cause and purpose.

Stop and think about the hygiene of your thinking most days. What thoughts do you think? Are they in the realm of your cause and purpose? Journal what occurs to you.

_____

_____

_____

_____

_____

_____

_____

Why the Word Cause and Purpose? Why Not Just One of Them?

Before we conclude this section, you might be wondering why the use of both words cause and purpose. Some of it comes from my faith belief that this life is just a dress rehearsal and that the work and talents we develop here will not fully manifest this side of eternity. Therefore, making good progress on my cause is about the best I can do before my spiritual graduation. Then, on the other side, my true purpose in all its glory will be revealed.

As I mentioned earlier, I love the word Teleios because one of the interpretations of the word is *the purpose beyond the purpose*. An example of this is what I just illustrated with the words cause and purpose. No matter your faith belief, the purpose beyond the purpose helps you understand and continue this quest with no finish line. There is no day when you can kick up your feet and say, "Aha! I think I have achieved my cause and purpose." The quest is never-ending, and it is as much about the journey as it is about any destination. There will be wins and wonderful moments, but they are fuel for the quest, not the end of it. Hence, I love cause and purpose as a lexicon because they point to the journey of leadership, of discovering our cause and purpose. At the same time, we are present in the moment, living whatever our understanding and version of it is at any given point.

One final thought on cause and purpose: when I think about the world filled with many living their cause and purpose, the visual that comes to mind that I pay forward to you is a lake. Picture the lake with a tranquil, calm surface, and then a gentle, sprinkling rain begins. As the raindrops hit the lake's surface, they create concentric circles emanating out. Other circles form, and those circles beautifully intersect. Can you see it in the theater of your mind? This visual illustrates great cause and purposes, living and intersecting. Let it be so in all our own lives.

Cause and Purpose

"A musician must make music, an artist must paint, a poet must write, if they are to be ultimately at peace with themselves."

Abraham Maslow

Questions to Ponder

- Do you have some sense of your cause and purpose? If not, I suggest these blogs to discover, wrestle with, and gain insight.
  - https://www.teleioscn.org/blog/the-dash-the-canvas-for-cause-and-purpose
  - https://www.teleioscn.org/blog/cause-and-purpose-the-7th-fundamental-of-every-great-organization-system
- A great cause and purpose should make the world better and change the trajectory of things. Does yours? How so?
- How can you grasp this on a daily basis? If you did, how would it change where you spend your time, how you spend your time, and how you utilize your time?
- Take some time now and wrestle with insight as to your cause and purpose. Here are some hints:

- Are there times when you perform your role or work on a certain type of project, and people affirm you, and you think, *really, that was nothing?* That is a hint to gifts you have.
- What makes you come alive?
- What experience have you gained on your journey so far? Are there themes amongst that experience?
- This life is an adventure; what adventure are you living in every aspect of your life?
- What visions do you have for your life, say ten years from now?
- Is there a movie that really touched something deep inside you? What was the movie? What was the storyline? Could this movie's storyline be a hint to your cause and purpose?
- Use all the above to help paint a picture and to put some words around your current understanding of your cause and purpose.

I want to challenge you by asking, "What are your cause and purpose? What has your adventure been like? What is your sense of what it is supposed to be like going forward?"

Stop now and use the space provided. Draw if you want to draw, write if you want to write. Do not try to edit it, and do not force it. What

Cause and Purpose

were you created to do? There may be several things. Take a deep breath, let it out, and take this space to capture what comes to you.

_____

_____

_____

_____

_____

_____

_____

_____

_____

_____

_____

_____

_____

"We do not burn out because of what we do, we burn out because we forget why we do it!"
Unknown

"What you leave behind is not what is engraved in stone monuments, but what is woven into the lives of others."
Pericles

Chapter 6: *Transition (SCII C&P)*

- **Self-Mastery**
- **Caring for Others**
- **Influence**
- **Intention**
- **Cause and Purpose**

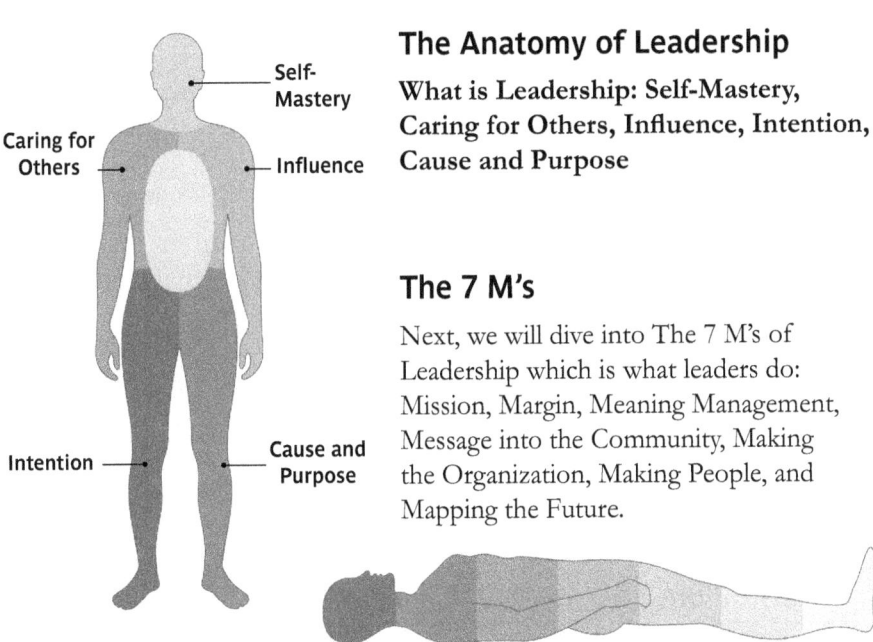

The Anatomy of Leadership

What is Leadership: Self-Mastery, Caring for Others, Influence, Intention, Cause and Purpose

The 7 M's

Next, we will dive into The 7 M's of Leadership which is what leaders do: Mission, Margin, Meaning Management, Message into the Community, Making the Organization, Making People, and Mapping the Future.

Dr. Thayer's definition of leadership was thought-provoking and somewhat poetic, and it bears repeating here in our transition to the 7 M's because it adds color and depth to our Anatomy of Leadership:

> **Leadership Defined**
>
> Leadership, from wherever it is exercised, has this universal characteristic: It changes the course of things…for the better IF worthy leadership, for the worse if not,
>
> Whether that is changing the course of a conversation,
>
> Or changing lives: yours first, then others, influencing how future lives will be lived, future perspectives altered,
>
> The performance of an organization or a piece of an organization…
>
> Of a gathering, a group, a community, a human endeavor (like music or marriage), or a whole society's trajectory.
>
> In other words, it changes the course of history, writ small or large—the history of a life, a relationship, a vocational domain, a community, or an organization.
>
> Without the intervention of competent leadership, things will simply evolve in the direction of the course they are on–teleologically. With worthy leadership, their trajectory is changed for the better, for all of those involved and thus for the larger social systems of which they are a part.
>
> ***So, by this measure are you a leader?***

If you rated yourself in the areas of the anatomy of a leader on a scale of 1 to 10, with 10 being masterful, how would you rate yourself in these areas?

Anatomy Category	**1 - 10 (Your Rating)**
Self-Mastery	_____
Caring for Others	_____
Influence	_____
Intention	_____
Cause and Purpose	_____

Give it a try; honestly assess yourself. Pay this assessment forward to a team member and have them rate themselves and you.

Create or edit your learning plan based on what you learn from this exercise (see Appendix 1). What "Aha's!" did you have as you read each chapter covering the anatomy areas above? Jot down some notes here and then codify those in your learning plan.

_____
_____
_____
_____

The Anatomy of Leadership

Remember Dr. Thayer's provocative statement about the only leaders of the 20th Century? That statement got me riled up; what about you? Do you watch the news or peruse social media and get mad at the state of our world, nation, state, or community? What about your team or your organization? Is there anything about them that riles you up just as much? Which is within your circle of influence and your circle of control?

Suppose we embodied or exemplified the five areas of The Anatomy of Leadership (self-mastery, caring for others, influence, intention, and cause and purpose) in the performance of our roles. In that case, I believe that when someone asks, "Who were the leaders of the 21st Century?" the answer would be that there were too many to count because they read this book and set out to change a team, a department, an organization, a family, or a community.

Given our definition of this anatomy, are you a leader? Are you up for the challenge?

As I conclude this first half of the book, I am reminded of my favorite movie, *It's a Wonderful Life*. We all know the plot line where George Bailey gets a glimpse of what the world would be like if he never was. Before that glimpse, he thought he was not living his cause and purpose. He missed the blessings all around him and how his life created a canvas for so many others around him to thrive. The same is true of you. Everyone has a cause and purpose, but few realize it, and few enjoy the journey of discovering and living it. Many people die at thirty and are buried at eighty-five. Discover your cause and purpose and live it. The world will be thankful one day if you are and that you did.

Stickiness in the Brain

In the book *Made to Stick* by the Heath Brothers, they identify a brilliant principle that great communicators create and package messages in such a way that they stick in our brains. Given the importance of leaders practicing leadership, I want The Anatomy of Leadership to be stuck in your brain. If you are like me, when you were in school, you used acronyms to memorize information. To this day, I can spell Mississippi due to this song my mom taught me:

M—I—cukkaletter—cukkaletter—I—cukkaletter—cukkaletter—I—humpback—humpback—I; Mississippi.

S—C—I—I—C&P
- S= Self-Mastery
- C= Caring for Others
- I = Influence
- I = Intention
- C&P = Cause and Purpose

In that spirit, SCII C&P is the acronym so you can remember The Anatomy of Leadership. Say it to yourself now: S—C—I—I—C&P. I am going for stickiness in our brains with this acronym. Did it work?

So now that we have the common ground of this thing called leadership, then what exactly do leaders do? That is where we will go next with the 7 M's of a leader.

"One can never consent to creep when one feels an impulse to soar."

Helen Keller

PART II
THE 7 M's

"A leader is one who knows the way, goes the way, and shows the way."

John C. Maxwell

Chapter 7: *Introduction to the 7 M's*

The Role of the Leader (*The 7 M's*): Mission, Margin, Meaning Management, Message into the Community, Making the Organization, Making People, and Mapping the Future.

One of our Teleios Team members said something that stuck with me and led to the 7 M's. She said, "Every CEO should focus on three M's: Mission, Margin, and Message." This really got me thinking because I often see CEOs and leaders struggling to define their roles. In that struggle, I sometimes see them default to what they know. This often puts them in swim lanes that affect the performance of the rest of their team and their entire organization. For example, from my experience, I am a CPA by trade and started my career in the finance department. My first C-suite role was as a CFO. When I first became a CEO, I naturally focused on the organization's financial health and came at every decision based on the financial implications. Nurses and social workers often default to this experience-based approach rather than fully encompassing their leadership roles. The 7 M's gives us a framework to ensure this does not happen. A based skill set is helpful, so I'm not recommending throwing the baby out with the bathwater. However, we should completely fill our toolbox with all the tools needed to be a high-performance leader.

Take a few moments and reflect. Where do you spend most of your time in your current leadership role? Think about the 7 M's: Mission, Margin, Meaning Management, Message into the Community, Making the Organization, Making People, and Mapping the Future. Are you trained in, and therefore naturally default to, that area? Jot down what comes to mind. Now, look at what you wrote. Is there a theme there? Do you see a competency or area you are comfortable with rather than what your organization needs? Are you aware of any gaps that nag at you that you know need to be covered in your organization?

Introduction to the 7 M's

_____

_____

_____

_____

_____

_____

_____

With these thoughts in mind, we will dive into the 7 M's. Be mindful of where you spend your time per your inventory above versus all the M's that need to be covered.

"Effective leadership is putting first things first. Effective management is discipline, carrying it out."

Stephen Covey

After my team member inspired me with three of the M's, I read and researched and concluded that there are 7 M's that every leader should be focused on regardless of their role. Some leadership positions might have a larger percentage of their time in a certain category, but each must spend some percentage in each of the 7 M's. Again, the M's are as follows:

- Mission
- Margin
- Meaning Management
- Message into the Community
- Making the Organization
- Making People
- Mapping the Future

Let's take each of them and go deeper.

"Leadership is the capacity to translate vision into reality."

Warren Bennis

"When imagination meets common purpose."

Barak Obama

Chapter 8: *Mission*

- **Mission**
- Margin
- Meaning Management
- Message into the Community
- Making the Organization
- Making People
- Mapping the Future

Your mission statement should be the magnetic north that a compass points to for your organization. If you know where the needle points on a compass, you know where you should go. I use the compass analogy rather than true north because magnetic north moves ever so slightly and interestingly over the course of time, and as you will see with the other M's, your mission will change over time if you want to stay relevant. The compass is an excellent analogy of what a mission statement could be for an organization. It is the ideal we strive for, and every day calls forward each of your team members to live it. It is the standard to compare each interaction. As you live it, you may find it shifts with time.

Dr. Thayer would call these interactions moments of truth. He would say, "Imagine yourself hovering above your organization, floating above the earth. You see snapshots, like the photographs on your cell phone, of your mission in action shown to you in thumbnail images. What do those snapshots, those moments of truth, tell you about the state of your mission?"

Take a moment to perform this visualization exercise. What do your moments of truth tell you about your team, department, or organization? Where did you smile as you imagined this? Where did you wince as you imagined this?

Mission

_____

_____

_____

_____

_____

_____

_____

Years ago, the leadership guru Peter Drucker wrote a book called *The Five Most Important Questions You Will Ever Ask About Your Organization.* The first question is, "What is our mission?" This does not necessarily mean that each leader should write a separate mission statement for their department or team, although there is nothing wrong with that. The bigger task here is to ensure that the organization's mission is relevant, given the current environment.

Jim Collins is one of my favorite authors, and in his book *Built to Last,* he points out the paradox of change and why magnetic north is a better analogy for mission than true north. "Indeed, the great paradox of change is that the organizations that best adapt to a changing world first and foremost know what should not change." This insight is critical to middle and intermediate-level leaders who may feel like they have a mission that is not keeping up with the changing marketplace or the changing needs of the area they serve.

Developing your Mission Statement

How can a team develop a mission statement that is relevant to the current environment? In our work at Teleios, I usually do not like to start with the mission statement. Ideally, we go with what is already in place. About two years into our work together is a much better time to wrestle with the relevancy of the mission statement. This is because leaders on the learning journey have a much better vantage point to craft a meaningful mission statement. However, you can craft a mission statement on day one if you are in the learning mode regarding:

- The market you intend to serve and the broader external factors influencing it.
- The customers you intend to serve and their goals.

Mission

- The workforce you have or intend to recruit; their competencies and needs.
- An in-depth understanding of the product or service you provide your customers.

Reconciling all this ensures you will ascertain the relevant information to develop your mission statement. Therefore, you can see why some learning on the journey is helpful.

However, now consider Steve Jobs. He understood what the customer wanted more than focus groups or an outside consulting firm. From the beginning, he had a strong sense of his mission. I can still remember how excited I got when I saved up and bought my first Sony Walkman, only to be disappointed in its performance. Jobs knew if he developed a sleeker tool that delivered music on demand, there would be a huge market for it. The result was the iPod, which eventually morphed into the smartphone, a product we cannot live without today.

We are not all Steve Jobs. His level of understanding of the market, where things were headed, what the workforce could deliver, and what the customer wanted may feel impossible to grasp fully. However, great teams have those puzzle-piece answers residing in their heads. If you recall the concept I shared in Chapter 6 from the Heath brothers' book

Made to Stick, the challenge is to get them out of our heads and to put the puzzle together in a cogent and sticky way.

"Employees want to believe their company has a meaningful purpose. They want to know that their own job is worthwhile. They want to make a difference. If all three of these conditions are accomplished, bottom line results will follow."

Quint Studer

The Current Reality of Your Mission Statement

Where are you with your current mission statement? Do you use it often? How relevant is it? As I stated earlier, Drucker's book *The Five Most Important Questions You Will Ever Ask About Your Organization* is a great book because it focuses on the basic questions you should know about your organization:

- What is our mission?
- Who is our customer?
- What does the customer value?
- What are our results?
- What is our plan?

Mission

Some of these questions will lead to several other M's, but the first three definitely speak to your ability to nail your organization's mission statement. Do you know the answer to these questions for your organization, team, or department? Take a few moments to jot down your answers here.

_____

_____

_____

_____

_____

_____

_____

How can you determine if you need an outside facilitator to help you and your team revisit or help craft your mission? If you are in charge of the process, you may not get to be a full participant in the process. In this case, it is helpful to have someone else facilitate. A facilitator can also push the team to dig deeper and discover more. Do you need a new, fresh perspective? Has your mission become stale? If yes, consider building a team together of key influencers in your organization and bringing in an outside facilitator to tackle updating or creating your mission statement.

Another helpful tool is Simon Sinek's Golden Circle. Often, mission statements devolve into what we do and how we do it, but the best mission statements nail the inside of the circle, which is why we do this work.

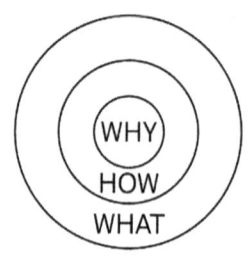

Here are some examples of some powerful mission statements:

Jet Blue: To inspire humanity—both in the air and on the ground.

Tesla: To accelerate the world's transition to sustainable energy.

TED: Spread Ideas.

LinkedIn: To connect the world's professionals to make them more productive and successful.

PayPal: To build the web's most convenient, secure, cost-effective payment solution.

Do any of these make you want to revisit your mission statement? I can remember wanting to revisit our mission statement when I was at Four Seasons. A friend of mine suggested I attend Pal's Center of

Mission

Excellence. Pal's is a hamburger and hot dog fast food restaurant in Eastern Tennessee. I know, hang with me as I had the same thought: *What could a hamburger and hot dog joint teach a hospice?* Well, I learned a ton. Pal's had won the Malcolm Baldrige Award, the highest quality award in the US. How a fast-food restaurant won such a prestigious award is a whole other story, but suffice it to say, I walked away from my two and a half days at their center of excellence full of ideas. One of the most profound things I witnessed was standing in one of their restaurants and watching 17ish-year-olds working together like a choreographed ballet. Each knew the mission statement, *Sudden Service* like it was emblazoned on their forehead.

I went back to Four Seasons and started asking if people knew our Mission Statement. It was over a paragraph long. What came out of that process was a new potent and powerful mission statement, *Co-creating THE care experience*. We used a video to roll out the new mission statement and included scenes where we asked people if they knew the old mission statement. The funniest line was a team member saying, "Ah, can I phone a friend?" It was a humorous way to poke fun at our old, irrelevant mission statement to pave the way for our new one.

Utilizing your Mission Statement

Once a leader is sure their mission is current and relevant, they must shout it from the mountaintops. Your mission statement should be referred to often, including when making difficult decisions. The mission statement should be woven into key moments of your organization, connecting those happenings to your magnetic north, your organization's reason for being.

At Teleios, we recently launched the annual *Care As It Should Be Award*, which recognizes moments in our network that illustrate care as it should be. The award represents our mission statement, giving us a tangible living way to reinforce our mission and even look for occurrences of it in action.

A benefit of writing this book is it has made me review how well I am modeling Teleios' mission statement in my own leadership. I recently sensed our team was tired, as many of them have been working long hours due to several big projects hitting at the busiest time of the year. The CEO of one of the hospices we work with shared an incredible story where a patient's dying wish was made possible by their hospice and that the hospice still exists due to their partnership with Teleios. I asked the CEO to attend our staff meeting and share this story as a Mission

Mission

Moment, which is how we refer to the beautiful stories that illustrate why we do this work. There wasn't a dry eye on the Zoom call, and at the end, I shared that the CEO said she would have thrown in the towel three years ago, but Teleios revived the wind in her sails for this sacred work we do. I let the impact of this settle on the team and then reminded them that this was our mission in action, *care as it should be*. I reminded each person that, no matter their role, they contributed to that Mission Moment, and if we were not doing the work we were doing, that Mission Moment may not have occurred. I meant every word, and each team member was touched by the weight of the story and the impact of the work we do.

Our mission statement would be just words without taking the time to connect everyone back to our why. Otherwise, the work can become just one task after another. I closed our time together by reminding our team that if we can connect what we are doing daily back to our why, we will not work another day in our lives. Instead, we will be living with cause and purpose. A mission statement properly crafted and utilized can do that for a team or organization.

How Mission Can Act as a Compass

Lastly, your mission statement can also be used as a plumb line or benchmark for the organization. Every action can be compared to the mission, and any deviation from it is an opportunity for improvement. Dr. Thayer used to say that the CEO hunts the status quo like it is the enemy. What he meant is that the CEO uses ideals such as the mission statement as the standard to challenge the organization to correct areas where we are not measuring up. Challenging the status quo ensures a constant recalibration to live your mission statement, just like a compass needle spinning and then pegging to magnetic north. Organizations and people drift; this is why a mission statement should be a living, breathing tool in the hands of leaders.

Once you have a great mission statement, you must ensure you and your team revisit it and utilize it daily.

What About Values

As I began to finish writing this book, I had the opportunity and challenge to present The Anatomy of Leadership at a conference. A good friend and mentor of mine, Mark Cohen, stood up and asked me a great question at the end of my presentation. "What about values?" I

Mission

Building Cathedrals

Three men, all engaged in the same employment, were asked what they were doing. One said he was making five dollars a day. Another replied that he was cutting stone. The third said he was building a cathedral. The difference was not in what they were actually doing, although the spirit of the third might quite possibly have made him the more expert at his task. They were all earning the same wage; they were all cutting stone; but only one held it in his mind that he was helping build a great edifice. Life meant more to him than to his mates because he saw further and more clearly. The farmer may be only planting seeds, but if he opens his eyes, he is feeding the world. The railroad man, and the factory hand, the clerk in the store, likewise are building their cathedrals. The investors in stocks and bonds, the executives of great corporations—they are building cathedrals likewise, if only they can catch the vision. The housewife does not count the dollars she receives for her exertions. If she did, her life would be unhappy indeed. The rest of us, the great figures of the industrial world more than the humble ones are thinking too much about such things as cutting stone and making profits, fully to be realizing the beauty of life.

Omaha Bee, *Leaves of Gold*

had thought about this but had failed to explain it in the book, so let me do so now.

Values are important and an essential tool in your toolbox as a leader. Values basically are ideals that we strive for towards one another as leaders and staff on a day-to-day basis.

John Maxwell would often say that he wanted to apologize for things he wrote about and how he performed his role in the past. I feel the same way. I can look back on my first time as Four Seasons CEO, and today, I want to apologize regarding how I fell short as a leader (I had the opportunity to be CEO twice, the second time being after my time with the Studer Group). However, the one exception that our team did very well was spend great time and care on what our values were and what they looked like in action. We would often use the phrase *our values in action*.

A powerful story of our values in action was our value of integrity. I would always meet with new employees within their first month at Four Seasons to talk about what our values looked like in action. A funny story I told repeatedly was how when we first rolled out our values, I was called on the carpet for the value of integrity. The story is when I first joined Four Seasons, we were not doing well financially. However, the state industry conference was being hosted in our city, which presented an excellent opportunity for staff training. We found out how many staff wanted to attend. It was beyond what we could afford, so I devised a creative solution. We had staff share registrations. Yeah, this sounds pretty bone-headed. Can you imagine if your name was Wendy, but your name tag said Rebekah, and someone approached you and said, "Hi, Rebekah?" But then you had to say, "Well, my name is actually Wendy, but my boss was too cheap to buy my registration." I wince as I type this, but it indeed happened.

When we rolled out the values, a staff member asked how that situation aligned with the value of integrity. So you know what I had to do? I had to apologize and own it. I then went on to recite this story as an example of the power of values. When behaviors don't line up, it does not matter if you are the CEO or the organization's receptionist; it is the ideal for our standards of behavior.

Well, this story has a Paul Harvey, *rest of the story* ending. My second time around as Four Seasons CEO, I told this story. At this point, the story was six years old, and something happened that never happened before. A new staff member was meeting with me as I reviewed our values. When I told this story, she stopped me and asked, "What did you do to make this right with the state association?" I was stunned; no one had ever asked me this before. God has an incredible sense of humor because, wouldn't you know it, the CEO of the state association was coming to Four Seasons that very afternoon. So I told him the entire story, almost cringingly.

He asked, "How long ago did this happen?" I told him over six years ago. He asked, "Why are you telling me this now?" I said, "Because a staff member called me on the carpet this morning, challenging me about making this right with the association." The story had an incredible ending as the CEO brought the state conference back to our city later in the year, and he asked that at least four of our leaders give presentations. That's the power of values in action. They are touchstones and ideals that we strive towards in our behavior. When we utilize them, great things happen as we compare what actually happens to those ideals.

But the question still stands: why did I not initially include values in the book? Well, certainly, it presents a problem that the word, values, does not start with the letter M, but there was a more significant issue. I realized upon reflection that I had bought into a key principle that Dr. Thayer taught. Dr. Thayer would often say the Mission is like Mother and he would paint in the air with his finger like an arch, an arch that stands above all. This emblazoned upon my mind that *the Mission stands above everything else*. It is Mother.

There is great wisdom here. The values are about how we treat each other, and you can do great things with a values-driven organization. However, values are horizontally focused, between you and me and between each other. The Mission is vertically focused. It is the overarching cause and purpose of why we are working together. Think about it in an important relationship like a marriage, for instance. If it is about you and your spouse or partner, that is awesome, and values are critical. However, if there is not a greater purpose for which you have come together, well, you might fall short of being a high-performance couple, team, or organization. *The Mission is mother and is our magnetic north. Values help us navigate the journey*, and I am glad Mark prodded me to add them. However, keep in mind that Mission trumps values in that values exist to support how we treat each other in our ever-striving towards the Mission.

Why the Mission is Like Magnetic North

When you use your mission statement this way, you may sometimes feel like you need to adjust it. In *Built to Last*, Jim Collins takes on the task of naming the principles for organizations built to last decades. Many of the hospices we work with in Teleios have served their communities for thirty or forty years. So how do we help capacitate them to be here another thirty or forty years? We loved the core analogy Collins shared in *Built to Last* so much that we incorporated it into our Teleios logo. He said, "The organization is somewhat like a hurricane. There is all this change and innovation swirling about, but in the middle, like the eye of the hurricane, is this somewhat unchangeable core, which is the organization's mission and values." This analogy seems to be teaching two opposing principles. The mission and the values anchor an organization. Still, by utilizing them as the core, almost like a center of gravity with all the change and improvement swirling about, the center itself may evolve with time. After more than thirty years of experience in business, I can see this principle in action.

In summary, the first M of the role of the leader is to ensure the mission is relevant and that the team stays on course with the mission each and every day by utilizing it as a tool, as a touchstone, as the needle on the compass to guide our journey.

"Our souls are not hungry for fame, comfort, wealth, or power. Those rewards create almost as many problems as they solve. Our souls are hungry for meaning, for the sense that we have figured out how to live so that our lives matter, so that the world will at least be a little bit different for our having passed through it."

Harold Kushner

Questions to Ponder

- How is your current mission statement? Does it inspire you and your team?
- Do you need a new mission statement?
- What will be your process to develop a new mission statement? How do you gather the wisdom of many team members and maybe even stakeholders?
- How will your mission statement guide decision-making within your organization?
- How will you communicate your mission statement to your employees, customers, and stakeholders?

- How will you ensure that your mission statement remains relevant and adaptable as your organization evolves?
- How will your mission statement help differentiate your organization from competitors?
- How will you ensure that your mission statement is reflected in your day-to-day operations and activities?
- How will your mission statement influence your long-term strategic planning?
- How will you incorporate your mission statement into your brand messaging and marketing efforts?
- How about values? Do you have values that are the ideals of how you and your team treat each other? If so, what is the relationship between your values and the mission of your organization? Is one referenced more often than the other? What might that tell you about the state of your culture?

_____

_____

_____

_____

Mission

"Measurement isn't the complete answer. The best groups measure, learn their lessons, then adjust, then review."

Max Depree

Chapter 9: *Margin*

- **Mission**
- **Margin**
- Meaning Management
- Message into the Community
- Making the Organization
- Making People
- Mapping the Future

The Anatomy of Leadership

My first executive position was as a CFO for a hospice in Pensacola, Florida. The CEO there had worked with Catholic Health Systems earlier in his career, and he taught me an adage I will never forget: *No margin, no mission.* The adage came from the nuns who were the administrators of Catholic hospitals in the 1960s, 1970s, and 1980s, and this wisdom pervades even today. The margin of an organization is the resources available to re-invest in the organization's mission. *The margin is a barometer of success or the lack thereof.* I will unpack this, but before I do, let me share a personal story of how hard this is to implement.

During my second week as a CFO, I was the first to find out that this hospice did not have enough money to make payroll. So, while they could repeat the adage, they had no concept of what it meant or how to put it into practice. I was not a clinician and did not have prior hospice experience, so I humbled myself and started to go out on patient visits and spend time with nurses and other hospice team members. They educated me, and at the same time, I educated them on how their day-to-day decisions impacted the organization's financial results. And guess what happened? In one year together, we turned that organization around financially. In some respects, it began my journey of being a Rosetta stone of sorts regarding what financials are and how to *un-complexify* (I made that word up) what seemed complex to most clinical leaders. Now, let's unpack what margin really is.

Margin Defined

So, what exactly is margin? First, let me offer this definition that will push your thinking, and then we will switch to a more technical explanation:

> **Margin**
> Margin is the current measure of inputs and outputs of a system, organization, team, or department. If there is a net positive gain, then you have a positive margin. If there is a negative gain, the system, organization, team, or department consumes more than it produces.

I know this is not the typical way to define margin. The usual CFO's definition is Net Revenue - Operational Expenses = Margin. Therefore, if your net revenue is $10 and your operational expenses are $7, your margin is $3. While this equation is true, accounting is one-dimensional, and leaders must be five-dimensional system thinkers (5D is beyond 3D). When thinking about organizational margin, the gain is the outcome of the leadership and teamwork that gets work done.

For example, my wife and I have five children. Our children are a blessing, and they are the product of two people coming together. Together we have produced more than we were individually. When thinking about your organization, team, or department, what are the inputs into the system? There are usually three:

- People
- Time
- Resources

What we do with these inputs will determine if there is a Return on Investment (ROI). At Teleios, we use ROI, Return on Effort (ROE), and Return on Attention (ROA) as lexicon tools to paint the picture of this concept.

When I worked with Dr. Thayer, he shared a concept called the Appreciated Value Index. He would say that each person in the organization should be able to have their own profit and loss (P&L) statement. This idea drove the accountants in the group crazy because they would say there was no way to account for all the inputs and outputs. The accountants were right, but they were missing Dr. Thayer's point and the actual lesson he was teaching.

That lesson was, what is the net impact of each leader on the organization or department? *Dr. Thayer also said each person should be worth about three times their salary to the organization.* I had never heard that before, but one of my favorite parables in the Bible is the "parable of the talents."

> **The Parable of The Talents (Matthew 25:14-30)**
> A man was going away on a journey. He called three of his servants together, and to the first he gave five bags of gold, to the second he gave two bags of gold, and to the third he gave one bag of gold. The first servant put the gold to work and produced five additional bags of gold. The second servant put the gold to work and produced two additional bags of gold. The third servant went and hid the gold in the ground. The master came back, and each servant had to give an account of what they did with their talents. The first two servants who gained more were given great rewards, but the third servant who hid his talents was thrown out and there was weeping and gnashing of teeth.

The punch line of the parable is startling. I mean, it is not like the third servant murdered someone or cheated someone. The servant simply did not produce a positive gain with what they were given. The parable is not an accounting lesson in scripture, but it is a life lesson. To whom much is given, much is expected! Great leaders take what is at their disposal and produce a positive outcome. Ideally, the goal is to produce three times what you are given, but even one or two times what you are given are incredible outcomes.

What is your salary? Multiply three times that amount. What number do you get? Ask yourself honestly, "Is your impact on the organization from your day-to-day work, leadership, communication, and energy producing that level of positive impact for your organization?" If the answer is yes, and more of your team members can say the same, you likely have an excellent margin for your organization. Have you seen this principle at play in your own life as well? Journal your thoughts about this.

_____

_____

_____

_____

_____

The More Common Definition of Margin

Here is Google's definition of margin:

> In the business world, the margin is the difference between the price of a product and the costs associated with making or selling the product (or the cost of goods sold). Broadly speaking, a company's margin is its ratio of profit to revenue.

Again, this is the typical one-dimensional traditional definition. However, if you can think about it in 3D, you will become a masterful leader and utilize margin as a measure of your success.

"Financial peace isn't the acquisition of stuff. It's learning to live on less than you make, so you can give money back and have money to invest. You can't win until you do this."

Dave Ramsey

Margin Re-imagined

Let me make one final attempt to push your thinking. In the future, those who can manifest ROI thinking, being, and doing will be the winners in any endeavor. Margin is a way of letting you know how good you are with ROI, ROA, and ROE thinking and competency. The financial measure is a lagging indicator when you are doing well. However, when you are performing poorly, it is a more immediate feedback tool. That might take a few moments to process. Think about your journey. Have you seen something similar at play but did not realize it at the time?

_____

_____

_____

_____

_____

_____

From my experience walking into some challenging financial situations, we had to buckle down and get clear about our inputs and outputs. We could not be fancy and focused on many things; instead, it often required saying no to some things we did before. Think of it like pruning a tree. This discipline moves the organization or department from a negative margin territory to about break-even (which means your margin is $0) or slightly better. It gets more complicated from here because the margin becomes more of a lagging indicator.

In our work at Teleios, we utilize the concept of Pillars because it gives more of a systems, or holistic, view of an organization. Service, Quality, People, Growth, sometimes Community, and then Finance are the categories, or Pillars, by which you need to look at your business. Managing all the Pillars concerning plans, inputs, priorities, and execution will have a long-term positive impact on your margin. (We will unpack Pillars more in Chapter 14.) At this point, the financial margin becomes a bit of a lagging indicator of the decisions you make and implement. Think of it like the wake of the ship. The ship is plowing through the water, and you are looking forward, making decisions, and implementing processes. As the ship plows through the water, it leaves a wake behind you. The wake is akin to your margin. It is a lagging indicator, but analyzing it is still helpful.

Where There's Smoke, There is Fire

What we have covered thus far should push your thinking. Now, we can return to the traditional way of looking at margin.

As I have said, I am a CPA by trade, but I am not your typical CPA. One thing I know from my years as a leader is that the numbers speak the truth, even when they are not totally accurate. Said another way, where there is smoke, there is fire. In my many years of experience, I have not met an organization that did not wish they had better data—more fine-tuned, detailed data. It can take many years of toil and effort to get those very detailed reports just how you want them. However, the wonderful thing about a margin is that you can screw up some of the detail amongst categories; however, the residual from your revenue minus your expenses is a great barometer and usually can be compared against peers. An organization should never let the lack of perfect data stultify them from religiously looking at their margin and asking questions regarding how they got there. As the adage goes, "All measuring is imprecise. Measure anyway."

"What you can't measure you can't manage."

Dr. Jay Kaplan

Margin

How much margin is enough? Well, the answer differs by organization. But here are some good questions to guide you:

- What is my industry average?
- Where are we intentionally (key word here) different, and should that degrade our margin, or should it bring in more increase to our margin?
- Where are we on our industry's life cycle (bell-shaped curve)?
  - If we are on the left side of the curve, margins will be smaller. This is an investment time and a great growth time for planting seeds and putting down roots that will potentially bear a great harvest in the future.
  - If we are on the top half of the curve, margins are strong. Strong margins mean harvest season, a good time to increase your reserves.

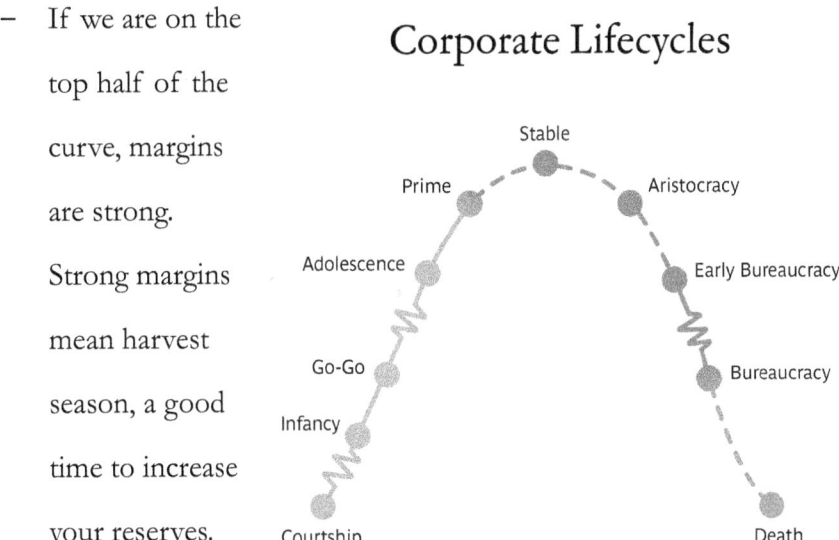

- If we are on the right side of the curve, then margins will really start to be squeezed, and cost-cutting will need to be a competency in your toolbox. This is a good pruning season, getting clear on what matters most while thinking about where we need to invest to position our organization for the future. Where are we going (this means mapping, which is one of the other M's we will unpack in Chapter 14), and what will the journey cost in terms of reserves (margin we have stored up)?

In summary, the second M of the role of the leader is to ensure we have a grasp on our margin, which is the gas in the tank to our mission and the gas we have in reserve. Leaders need to understand and have competency regarding the ins and outs of margin. They should be fully involved in answering questions to help the broader team understand the margin. All leaders should be teachers regarding the inputs and outputs of the organization's margin and why it is so important. Remember, ROI, ROE, and ROA thinking are foundational to success in this area. As you get better and better with margin, you can gain more confidence by looking at the prow of the ship and making decisions, knowing how they will register in the wake of the ship (i.e., the margin).

Margin

"Money is a terrible master but an excellent servant."

P. T. Barnum

Questions to Ponder

- Do you understand the components that determine your organization's margin?

- Do you understand the difference between your operating margin and your overall bottom line net income or net loss?

- Does your team understand the concept and, more importantly, the practice of creating a return on investment from the decisions being made?

- Have you allowed a lack of technical or financial knowledge to prohibit you from understanding this chapter's basic concepts? How can you remedy that starting tomorrow?

- Where is your organization on the bell-shaped curve by your various service lines? Given your plotting on the curve, what does that mean concerning where you need to place bets on time, energy, and financial resources?

The Anatomy of Leadership

"Without good communication, a relationship is merely a hollow vessel carrying you along on a frustrating journey fraught with the perils of confusion, projection, and misunderstanding."

Dr. Chérie Carter-Scott

Chapter 10: *Meaning Management*

- **Mission**
- **Margin**
- **Meaning Management**
- Message into the Community
- Making the Organization
- Making People
- Mapping the Future

The Anatomy of Leadership

I learned the concept of *meaning management* from Dr. Lee Thayer, who won a lifetime achievement award as a pioneer in communication. Many of us have been trained to believe that communication is all in what we say and how we say it. While this is true, Dr. Thayer flipped the communication paradigm around, teaching that where the proverbial rubber meets the road is how the person receiving the information interprets it. Therefore, how do we do a better job of managing the meaning of things?

First, know that meaning management is not about controlling the meaning of things because that approach leads to a bad culture. For example, if you approach communication that way, people will see it for what it is—spin. The reality and the intentionality of communication, the words chosen (i.e., the lexicon), the stories told, and the symbols and pictures used all either confirm the meaning being managed, or they do not. If they do not, your culture is going to have issues.

Managing meaning is really about intentionality in communication. I have been in many types of organizations over the years, and one of the first things I do is listen to the language people use. If the organization is very loose with its language, it tells me a lot about how intentional they are with other things. An organization with its own language, an intentional way of saying things meaningfully, usually has a healthier culture that translates into high performance in all aspects of the organization, especially in delivering its mission. All of this equals meaning management, which connotes an active, ongoing, never-ending process.

Creating this type of culture is hard work. It takes time to be intentional with language. The team has to come to work every day in learning mode, once again, hunting the status quo and the cliché like it is the enemy. As a leader, asking questions is a great way to help manage the meaning of things because questions make others think more deeply about things. As a result, the meaning is better managed. The analogy I think of is like the older days when we had dial-up internet via America On-Line. The modem would make this shrill noise, and then the modem on the other end of the line would make a shrill noise as they synced up to receive and transfer information. Meaning management is somewhat like that wherein questions and discussion create a syncing process. However, it is better than the modem analogy because it is not just about receiving and sending information. Higher level communication happens when sending and receiving information and asking questions produce something that did not exist before: understanding, ideas, creativity, and actions. This activity is the ongoing creative process of meaning management.

"The meaning of communication is the response and resulting actions you get."

Dr. Lee Thayer

Thought Prodders to Go Deeper on Meaning Management

Below are ideas and prodding questions to help with meaning management. They get to the heart of how you and your team can improve your competency in meaning management.

First, you can only know what you are capable of knowing. If you are not competent in a subject, engaging in effective communication and meaning management will be difficult. Therefore, the first step is to gain more experience with the subject matter. W. Edwards Deming would say if you cannot describe what you are doing in simple terms, you probably do not know what you are doing. Ponder that for a second. What "Aha's!" come to you about things you have been attempting to communicate in an area of your life?

Meaning Management

_____

_____

_____

_____

_____

_____

_____

Second, what you know is limited by the words and ideas you regularly consume. How does this apply to meaning management?

If your vocabulary is limited, effectively managing the meaning of things will be difficult. To clarify, meaning management is not about using fancy words. Some of the best communicators are more storytellers than walking dictionaries. How is your linguistic toolbox? Can you paint the picture with words? How accomplished are you at leading your team step-by-step through complex ideas? Ponder these questions. Do you have any "Aha's!" regarding opportunities for improvement?

The Anatomy of Leadership

_____

_____

_____

_____

_____

Third, you cannot know everything. How does this apply to meaning management?

Acknowledging that you cannot know everything is an important point that will allow you to take a deep breath. There is a book recently written called *The Information Diet*. Have you considered there is more information available now than ever before in the history of mankind? You cannot know everything, nor should you. So, what does your role require? This gives you a good swim lane to focus on what you need to know for your role. The more you master the material in your area of expertise, the better communicator and meaning manager you can become. As you ponder this quandary, are there areas that are in your swim lane for your role where you need to focus more on your learning efforts? Journal your thoughts.

Meaning Management

_____

_____

_____

_____

_____

_____

_____

Fourth, what you know becomes part of who you are, and who you are is immensely resistant to change. How does this bear on meaning management?

- How are you when dealing with change?
- If you are naturally resistant to change, how does your communication typically come across regarding items where change is needed? Is it dramatic?
- Are you overly concerned about the change? How does it impact others?
- What is your intended impact? How would you know?

The Anatomy of Leadership

_____

_____

_____

_____

_____

_____

I recently worked with someone naturally good with details. However, they were not aware that their default response to change was to sound overly concerned. This reaction to change was detrimental to others grasping the need to know to move things forward. Could this be said about you?

When our kids were growing up, my wife and I would challenge them to think about something and not just say there is no way to do it. To make that point, we would sing the nursery rhyme, *There's a Hole in My Bucket*, so the children would think past the challenges to find solutions. Here are some of the lyrics:

> There's a hole in my bucket, dear Liza, dear Liza,
> There's a hole in my bucket, dear Liza, a hole.

Meaning Management

Then mend it, dear Henry, dear Henry, dear Henry,

Then mend it, dear Henry, dear Henry, mend it.

With what shall I mend it, dear Liza, dear Liza?

With what shall I mend it, dear Liza, with what?

With straw, dear Henry, dear Henry, dear Henry,

With straw, dear Henry, dear Henry, with straw.

The straw is too long, dear Liza, dear Liza,

The straw is too long, dear Liza, too long.

Then cut it, dear Henry, dear Henry, dear Henry,

Then cut it, dear Henry, dear Henry, cut it.

With what shall I cut it, dear Liza, dear Liza?

With what shall I cut it, dear Liza, with what?

With a knife, dear Henry, dear Henry, dear Henry,

With a knife, dear Henry, dear Henry, a knife.

The knife is too dull, dear Liza, dear Liza,

The knife is too dull, dear Liza, too dull.

Then sharpen it, dear Henry, dear Henry, dear Henry,

Then sharpen it, dear Henry, dear Henry, sharpen it.

With what shall I sharpen it, dear Liza, dear Liza?

With what shall I sharpen it, dear Liza, with what?

With a stone, dear Henry, dear Henry, dear Henry,

With a stone, dear Henry, dear Henry, a stone.

The nursery rhyme continues until finally returning to, "There's a hole in my bucket…"

I even introduced this nursery rhyme to my team and refer to it at home and work when we sense someone is either lazy with their thoughts or simply resistant to change without being thoughtful regarding the issue. All it takes is a simple phrase, "There's a hole in my bucket, dear Liza…"

How about you? Can you think of a time when you defaulted in a situation, were resistant to change, or went on screen saver mode rather than engaging in the conversation thoughtfully? How did that impact the meaning of things?

_____

_____

_____

_____

_____

Fifth, we are the average of the people we hang around. Who are you hanging around, and how are they impacting you? I paid this lesson forward to all five of my kids. I remember when our oldest, Ian, had to deliver something to me while I was in class at the Thayer Institute. Dr. Thayer asked Ian to step in front of the whole class. Then he asked, "What is one thing your dad has taught you?"

Ian is naturally introverted, but he did not miss a beat. He said, "You are the average of the people you hang around." Dr. Thayer smiled because he often said, "If you want to be a straight-A student, hang out with the straight-A students. If you want to be a B or C student..." Well, you know the rest.

I was already proud of Ian's answer, but he continued, "At my college, there are not many straight-A students, so I find myself hanging out with the older adults who have gone back to school to better themselves." It is awesome when your kids are teaching you.

So how about you? Who are the people in your circle? Do they make you better? What is the quality of your conversations? Do you see this principle at play in your own life?

_____

_____

_____

_____

_____

_____

Use these thought prodders to help you think more deeply about your ability to manage the meaning of things. Pay it forward so that it is truly heard by your team members. Meaning management is hard stuff.

Are We Really Communicating? How Would You Know?

The Irish playwright George Bernard Shaw said, "The single biggest problem with communication is the illusion that it has taken place." In other words, if our trust in whether we communicated is in what we said, then we are missing a large part of the equation. Dr. Thayer would often use the term, *managing the meaning of things*.

Meaning Management

Unfortunately, we have grown so cynical in our twenty-four-hour news cycle that when we hear this phrase, we think it is spin.

As I have stated earlier, managing the meaning of things is an active, ongoing process and is very dynamic. Dr. Thayer often saw sloppy, unintended communication costing organizations time, money, and talent. In fact, he said seventy percent of all organizational costs were due to ineffective communication. I thought he was overly dramatic when he said this, but the more I live, learn, and work with different organizations, including my own, I see this principle at play. It may not be seventy percent, but I'm sure it exceeds fifty percent of all costs, especially unintended costs, which negatively impacts the margin of the organization.

In most organizations, ineffective communication leads to layer upon layer of departments due to ineffective communication. Interestingly, this only compounds the problem of communication. The ideal organization effectively manages the meaning of things and develops a lexicon with well-intended, well-thought-through definitions for concepts and things that are important to the organization. The result is an efficient, reasonably flat organization where people know their roles and communicate their critical need to know to one another.

The Anatomy of Leadership

During orientation at Teleios, we give our new team members a sheet with definitions of words that are part of Teleios' lexicon. We begin to manage the meaning of things from day one of a new team member's employment. The challenge with this tool is that it must be updated frequently because the lexicon is alive and constantly evolving. Our tech team understood this and created a wiki-type function to harvest and update the lexicon sheet in close to real-time.

I shared the *cat analogy* with you in the preface of this book. This analogy is an effective tool to ensure people manage the meaning of things and acts as a thought prodder of sorts for when we are not. I use it even in my personal relationships because people frequently nod their heads, thinking that they are talking about the same thing. However, they are really understanding and thinking very different things. They assume they are synced up when, in fact, they are far from it.

I observed this in my own organization recently in a planning session. One team member *set the table* for their comments. *Setting the table* is another excellent tool for managing the meaning of things. I was tracking with the employee, but one comment from another team member told me that they were interpreting what was just set on the table in a completely different way. The employee went on to recommend a significant change to a training we provide at Teleios, a training that is one of the best I have seen and majorly impactful to others. It has evolved over the years into effective training because we listen to our attendees, discern their feedback, and adjust what we teach based on what we learn from the input. I then asked that employee, "When was the last time you went through the training?" The answer was five years ago. If we had taken this employee's recommendation at face value, we may have harmed something with great value in what we do today. Interestingly, I still harvested a pearl in this employee's comments that will help us better explain how we have evolved this training. That is the beauty of robust communication; even when it is imperfect, there are things to learn.

The Ultimate Meaning of Things

Dr. Thayer often said, "We create our existence in our communication." Ponder this for a moment. Your existence is created in the words you use and in what you communicate. What about the organizations you know? Can you see this at play with them? Not grasping this principle is why most organization's efforts to improve communication do not make meaningful progress.

The Anatomy of Leadership

I once witnessed a long-time student of Dr. Thayer's meet with his senior team to discuss the recent employee engagement survey results. The team shared that the survey demonstrated they had communication issues. The CEO repeatedly said, "No, we don't have communication issues." The team pushed back and said, "But the survey says we do." It was like watching a ping-pong match. I was intrigued because I knew this CEO to be very bright and open in his leadership style. It did not make sense that he was denying the existence of an issue. As I watched the exchange, I realized that he was brilliantly pushing his team's understanding of the real issue. It was a great demonstration of meaning management. It was the *5 Why's* without using the word *why*.

There have been times when I have found myself accepting the status quo and not pushing in on meaning management. A scenario like this results in the team running off to create big projects such as an organizational newsletter or something that takes a lot of energy and effort.

> **The 5 Why's**
> The *5 Why's* is a concept taught by Toyota that utilizes the word "Why" five times in the course of a discussion to push people to get to the real center, core, or meat of an issue rather than allowing team members to stay out on the periphery.

Meaning Management

However, because we did not truly understand the core of the problem, communication did not improve. The lesson my friend was teaching is similar to the *5 Why's*. He was trying to get to the heart of where the real communication challenges lay. It was a masterful performance, and the lesson was not lost on me.

One of my team members gave me a short but brilliant book called *Hung by the Tongue*. The entire book brought to light the power in the words we use. Francis P. Martin, a Cajun pastor from Louisiana, wrote the book. He quoted many scriptures that illustrate the principle Dr. Thayer shared regarding how we create our existence in words. Here is my interpretation:

The world we create is built, defined, and interacted with based on the words we use, how we use them, and their impact on others.

In the movie *Inception*, the characters create cities and even a world in their dreams where they exist and interact; this is what I am going for with the word *define*.

This makes me think much more deeply and intentionally (there is that word again) about my communication, thoughtfully choosing words and using stories and illustrations to manage the meaning of things better. Also, the context is essential: what is my cause and purpose and the cause and purpose of the person with whom I am communicating? The communication will move us closer or farther away from those intended destinations.

Before I learned about managing the meaning of things, I think much of my communication was purposeless. Today, I can barely tolerate idle chit-chat. An illustration of this is when people arrived at class, they would ask Dr. Thayer, "How are you today, Dr. Thayer?" Many of us are asked that daily, and we say, "Fine, how are you?" It is all a waste of oxygen as we are not even present in the discussion. Our minds are a million miles away thinking about something else while our tongues are spouting platitudes and cliches. Dr. Thayer often answered, "I don't know, how about you tell me." It was a brilliant way of shaking the cobwebs off the other person and saying, "Are we going to have meaningful, purposeful communication here, or are we going to play silly games using words neither of us means?"

"People only see what they are prepared to see."

Ralph Waldo Emerson

The Meat of Meaning Management

This takes us to the meat of meaning management. The concept of meaning management is a lexicon and framing around communication, giving you a better chance of having more effective communication. Without this framing, you could just be chasing your tail, and since time is our most precious resource, I definitely do not want you doing that.

I am not a huge *Star Trek* fan, but it contains a wonderful analogy for meaning management. Wouldn't it be great if the Vulcan Mind Meld was real? Could you imagine if we could download into each other's brains what we needed to know? There is a great scene in the movie *The Matrix* where the character Trinity climbs into a helicopter, and Neo, the hero of the story, asks, "Do you know how to fly this thing?" She responds, "Not yet." Over her headset, she asks their controller to download the helicopter protocol into her brain. Her eyes flutter, and suddenly, she knows how to fly a helicopter. If it was only that easy.

Short of that future innovation, what we can do is build a better lexicon in our organization and teams, find out what we need to know to play our roles as efficiently as possible, and then communicate that effectively and in such a manner that creates meanings that did not exist before. These steps are the essence of meaning management. Do not forget the importance of storytelling and illustrations as crucial methodologies to do a more efficacious job in meaning management.

The third M, meaning management, is challenging but necessary for a leader to truly become a leader. To draw from the *moments of truth analogy* mentioned in Chapter 8 on Mission, those moments of truth are a great barometer of how well we have managed the meaning of things.

"The story you tell yourself is often a stormy first draft."

Brenee' Brown

Questions to Ponder

- How good of a communicator are you currently? How would you know?
- How can understanding the concept of meaning management help you to communicate more effectively in your personal and professional relationships?
- How can you ensure your message is received and interpreted as intended?

Meaning Management

- How can you use the concept of meaning management to enhance your listening skills and better understand the messages of others?
- Do you know how your empathy and emotional intelligence affect your communication skills? Once you gain better self-understanding, can you see how your prior ways impacted your communication and how well you manage the meaning of things?
- How good are you and your team at utilizing questions to probe deeper and have more meaningful discussions?
- Do you hunt the cliché like it is the enemy? In other words, how often do you, as the leader, push in and ask people, "What did you mean by that?" You will be surprised how often people use platitudes when they do not mean them or have no intention behind them.
- Does your team or organization have a lexicon of commonly used, intentionally defined words? If not, feel free to contact me, and I can share our Teleios lexicon as a starter set. Note: The words in our lexicon are not plug-and-play. You will need to debate them and discuss them with your team so they will truly own them. Once you do that, then you can call them your own lexicon.
- How can you effectively adapt your communication style to engage with different audiences and situations?

- How can you use technology and digital communication tools to improve communication?
- How can you develop a culture of effective communication within your team, organization, or community?
- How can you continue to develop and refine your communication skills over time?

_____

_____

_____

_____

_____

_____

_____

_____

_____

"In this ever-changing society, the most powerful and enduring brands are built from the heart. They are real and sustainable. Their foundations are stronger because they are built with the strength of the human spirit, not an ad campaign."

Howard Schultz

Chapter 11: *Message into the Community*

- **Mission**
- **Margin**
- **Meaning Management**
- **Message into the Community**
- Making the Organization
- Making People
- Mapping the Future

The Anatomy of Leadership

Recently, we did an assessment of an organization. The CEO had just retired, and the organization was looking for a replacement. Every senior leader said the new CEO should be *our face to the community*. While this is important, it is only one small sliver of what the CEO should be. The CEO should be much more than just a face in the community.

Years ago, I read a great article by the CEO of Procter and Gamble, A. G. Lafley, titled "What Only the CEO Can Do." Lafley stated, "Conventional wisdom suggests that the CEO is primarily a coach and a utility infielder, dropping in to solve problems where they crop up. However, the CEO has a very specific job that only they can do: *link the external world with the internal organization*. It is a job that only the CEO can do because everybody else in the organization focuses much more narrowly and almost always internally. It's a job the CEO must do because there is no inside without the outside." The concept he is getting at is filling in what messaging into the community can and should be.

Messaging into the community is more than being a face to the community. It is also being the ear, harvester, and interpreter of:
- What the community is saying
- What are the community's current and future needs?

- What are the community's goals?
- How does all of the above reconcile with what we are providing today and anticipating we will provide tomorrow?

A Mental Visual of What Message of the Community Could Be Like

While the Lafley article focuses on the CEO's role in relation to messaging into the community, no CEO can be that good and in that many places at once. Therefore, this M applies to all the leaders in the organization.

Years ago, there was a movie starring Michael Douglas called *The Ghost in the Darkness* about a group of people on a safari. During the movie, the lions flip the script and begin to hunt the safari party instead of the other way around. There is a great scene in the movie where the whole camp had to sleep shoulder to shoulder in a circle, looking outside the camp. This scene is a great metaphor that together, the organization's leaders should have a 360-degree purview out into the community. It also illustrates how hard it is to message into the community.

At Teleios, we coach the organizations we work with to track their referral sources to determine what the hospitals are saying, what our nursing center partners are saying, and what the community is saying. All leaders should have pieces and parts of the story like everyone has a key puzzle piece. When the puzzle is put together, the picture this information paints enables the organization to message into the community.

When I first started at Four Seasons, we had a hospice house that was providing residential care similar to what an assisted living facility would provide. Many things were happening in our community, impacting the availability of beds where a much higher level of care could be provided. Therefore, we went through a process to convert those beds to be more like our hospice hospital beds, beds where we could get patients' pain and symptoms under control so they could return home and live their final months. Interestingly, we over-extrapolated the need for those beds and ended up with about six more beds than needed several years later. We used the rooms as office space, and then a few years ago, when the COVID-19 pandemic hit, we retrofitted the space into rooms to care for COVID-19 hospice patients. I don't mean this to be a lesson in technical healthcare but rather an example demonstrating that messaging into the community is ongoing and never-ending. What does the community need, and what are we providing?

Message into the Community

To use a football analogy, the final five yards of messaging into the community that we may forget is how to message back into the community so the community knows that you listened and have available what they need or may need.

Triangulation, A New Way to Understand This Word

Another concept that helps in understanding messaging into the community is the term Dr. Thayer called *triangulation*. You must erase the whiteboard on the negative connotation where we currently think that triangulation is akin to the drama triangle between people. This definition is different and speaks to the dynamic process of hearing the community and reconciling what you hear to what your organization provides.

Here is an analogy I came up with after learning this concept that helped me visually get my mind wrapped around triangulation as a key tool in messaging into the community. Think of a submarine that is tracking a ship. The submarine sends out a ping to find the ship's location. The ping hits the ship and bounces back, giving the submarine the data. Based on that data, the submarine must calculate and anticipate where the ship will be to fire its torpedo. This is a dynamic, three-dimensional process.

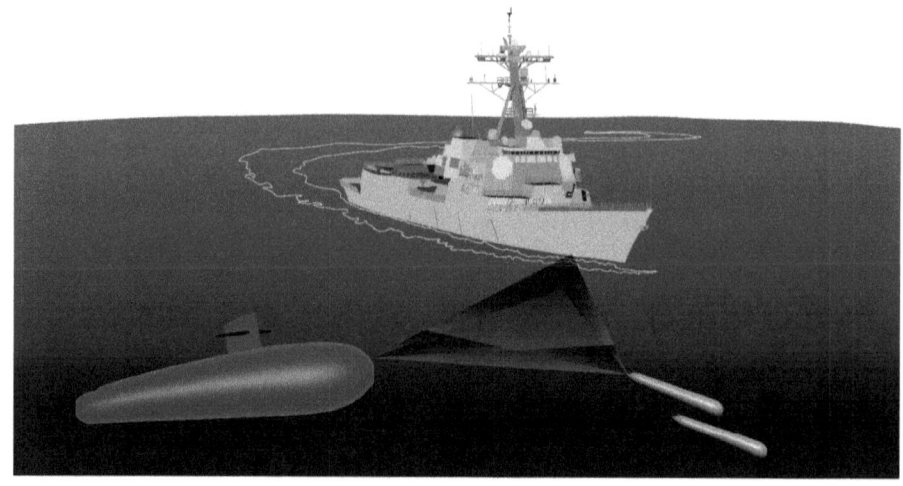

In this context, triangulation gives you an image of the multi-dimensional process of messaging into the community and how hard it is to assess what the community or your customer needs while reconciling this to what your organization provides.

Based on this definition, how are those moments of truth in action working for your organization, and more importantly, how is this working for the community and those you serve?

For the purposes of this book, I mean community in the broadest sense; not just your immediate community where your organization lives and serves, but also the state community that impacts our mission and even the national and global community.

"A CEO must be able to connect with employees, customers, and stakeholders on an emotional level to build trust and loyalty."

A.G. Lafley

Messaging Into the Community

Recently, our national organization engaged a highly creative marketing group to research end-of-life care and craft messaging that would help the triangulation process. Fascinating information emerged from this process, such as how mistrustful the public has become regarding the broader healthcare system. What do we do with that information? For years, leaders in the hospice space have thought we need to become respected and paint the picture we are part of the healthcare system. That is a heavy lift and requires strategic positioning and smart marketing, and then (Bam!) you find out this change could harm the brand and perception you have spent years building. Therein lies the challenge of messaging into the community; it is ever-evolving, which is what the triangulation concept depicts.

> ### Go to Gemba
>
> Years ago, I hardwired an annual practice where I take one to three days and go out on patient visits. The Japanese coined the term *Gemba walk*, which loosely translated means go see for yourself. Until the COVID-19 pandemic, I kept to this practice annually because it gave me a very tangible way to hear from the customer, see what our organization was providing, and determine how well the two matched. Data can help in this area, but that is still one-dimensional. The moments of truth analogy used earlier is a robust ideal of what you would hope you could access for your organization to see what the external world is seeing and saying regarding what you are providing. You should also start to see how all the M's relate to one another as messaging into the community also applies to your mission. Your margin is a barometer of sorts, and meaning management out into the community also helps complete the triangulation process.

Several of the hospices we work with, via Teleios, engaged an external firm to conduct customer focus groups, a smart way to get feedback. Those sessions were taped, and I watched many of them and gleaned pearls of information. It was like a recorded example of the moments of truth concept I shared earlier, with critical data points to ensure our message into the community was on target.

Sometimes, It Is Like Magic

In Chapter 8, Mission, I shared how Steve Jobs had a gift few possess. He had a sense that the iPod was what the customer wanted and needed. You could say Jobs was a magician, and what he did was pure magic, or at least he carried that persona. In reality, he was very attuned to the customer and was always looking and learning (i.e., practicing messaging into the community). He saw how we all loved and hated our Sony Walkman's and how they fell short of what they could have been. They applied Apple's cool design competency and their vision of changing the world, and what started as the iPod is now our smartphone, and our music and everything else is on the phone that we carry with us everywhere.

What is the magic you and your team could provide for the world by listening and being attuned to what the customer wants and by getting really good at messaging into the community?

_____

_____

_____

_____

_____

_____

_____

_____

_____

In summary, messaging into the community is multi-dimensional in its aspects, but the sum of it all is:

How well is what we are providing meeting the needs of those we serve? If what we are providing is falling short, how do we begin the process to harvest what the customer wants compared to what we

_____

"A CEO's most important job is to develop a shared vision and set of values that everyone in the organization can believe in and work towards."

Jack Welch

_____

provide? How do we then send messaging back out to let the customer know we have what they desire or are going to desire?

Questions to Ponder

- Do you know how well what your organization is currently providing is meeting the needs of your customers and your stakeholders?
- If that question made you uncomfortable, how can you and your team increase your organization's competency in knowing where the gaps are?
- Once you have identified those gaps, what should you do with that information?
- What processes or service lines are in place that those answers should impact?
- How well does your messaging back into the community let your customers know you have what they need? How would you know if it does?
- What three things can you do in this area of messaging into the community in the next month to move this concept forward?

The Anatomy of Leadership

"People want to be on a team. They want to be part of something bigger than themselves. They want to be in a situation where they feel that they are doing something for the greater good."

Mike Krzyzewski

Chapter 12: *Making the Organization*

- **Mission**
- **Margin**
- **Meaning Management**
- **Message into the Community**
- **Making the Organization**
- Making People
- Mapping the Future

The Anatomy of Leadership

Messaging into the community naturally leads us to the next M, making the organization. Messaging into the community is one of the more difficult roles of a leader. Even if you do this incredibly well, you will still fall short if you do not compose your organization properly to meet the community's needs via your mission.

According to Dr. Lee Thayer, organization-making is one of the primary ongoing tasks of a leader. He meant that the task of composing the organization is never-ending. Most leaders do not understand this. We often default to typical roles, such as, "I need HR, I need a CFO, etc." Relevant questions to determine the team for making the organization include:

- Who is on our team?
- What role will they play?
- What is their superpower?
- What roles do we need for the future?
- What skills will we need for the future?
- What is the mission and vision we are working to achieve?
- What did we learn with Messaging into the Community?
- What is our plan to get there?

Making the Organization

Jot down your answers.

Determining an organization's answers to the questions above is challenging but necessary to navigate the future. I have re-engineered a Jack Welch quote that gets behind the *why*, "If the external rate of change is greater than the internal rate of learning, we are screwed." The learning mode is necessary for any organization and even more so for one that aspires to be a high-performance organization. How the organization is composed is critical. Here are some great questions to provoke thinking around organization-making:

- How will decisions be made given where we are headed as an organization?
- Do we have all the skills we need to navigate the future?
- How does the team play together on a day-to-day basis in executing our plan?
- What skills are we missing, and can we learn those skills via internal resources, or do we need an external resource to help us cover that gap?

Making the Organization = Composing the Organization

I love the term composing the organization because composing music is a fitting metaphor. I am not musical, but I have talked to gifted musicians. They describe composing music as a multi-dimensional process whereby you have a sense of where you are trying to go and compose the music to get you there. Composing a team is similar. You must have a sense of where you are headed, what the community or customer values are, and what skill sets and roles will be needed to get you there. Most leaders go about this conventionally, thinking, " I need an HR person, a finance person, and an operations person." While that may be true at some level, for a high-performance organization, you should cast roles necessary for the story to unfold as intended or envisioned. If not, you will get a very conventional team and, more than likely, a very conventional outcome.

The Anatomy of Leadership

"Combining everyone's knowledge begets more knowledge, the way combining rice and beans begets more protein."

Elizabeth Hilts

The following is an example of making the organization that may resonate. When my kids were younger, I would coach their teams so I could be more present with them. I found myself coaching football. Luckily, I played and studied football, so that was no problem. However, I also coached sports I had never played, like soccer. A friend gave me great advice, "At this age, the kids only need three skills: running downfield, kicking, and stopping the ball at the goal." At the first practice, I broke the game down into those three skills, and then I asked the kids what was their superpowers. I love kids because they are often still very in touch with their purpose, gifts, and the joy of life. Many raised their hands and shared: I am fast, a good kicker, a great encourager. Just like that, I had all the pieces of the puzzle to compose my kid's soccer team. And guess what? We won most of our games.

Another tip a friend gave me is that young kids love animals, especially tigers. We used the analogy that a great goalkeeper was like a tiger because they pounced on their prey. Most kids wanted to play goalie to play the role of a tiger. We hardly had any goals scored on us the whole season. This analogy brings us to a vital tool in composing the organization: the role description.

Role Descriptions

We introduced the concept of a role description in Chapter 4. Now is a great time to revisit that tool. A role description is not a job description. It is the role that needs to be played to help the organization realize its destiny or cause and purpose. Part of composing the team is developing role descriptions for each team member.

Think of it this way: what is your favorite movie? Write the name of the movie and your favorite character below.

_____

_____

_____

My favorite movies are *Braveheart*, *Forest Gump*, and *Gladiator*. In each movie, if you took out the main characters of William Wallace, Forest Gump, and Maximus, or even some supporting characters, the

Excerpt From My Role Description At Teleios

- Your role is to be the conductor of the orchestra for all Teleios' activities.

- Your role is to be the chief recruiter and organization composer to build and develop a team (making people) and to ensure their competence to provide value-added products/solutions, support services, and subject matter specialist coaching for Serious Illness Care. Your role is to be the Teleios culture cultivator, ensuring Teleios' culture is fluid and dynamic in order to accomplish our vision, plan, and mission.

- Your role is to be the chief steward of our budget and balance sheet to ensure our mission and vision continue far into the future in accordance with our operational plan and strategic plan.

- Your role is to be the chief strategy practitioner who helps *uncomplexify* our vision and our plans to ensure they are dreamed, vetted, and either moved forward or discarded (with learning). Your role is to be the Teleios organization plan architect, organizer, and provoker. Your role is to be a coach to the Teleios team.

Note: See Appendix 2 for a complete example of my role description.

Making the Organization

stories would not be the same, and the outcomes of the storyline would not come to fruition. This is what a role description does. It gives a vision of the role that someone is to play. If the role is not played, the story never plays out as intended or envisioned.

Take some time now and think about your role description. What elements do you need to include?

_____

_____

_____

_____

_____

_____

_____

Role descriptions are tools that aid in the process of making the organization or composing the organization. Critical components for developing a role description include understanding the mission of what we are to do on a daily basis and then the vision of where we are going (that's the 7th M, which we will get to in Chapter 14), and then composing the organization with team members that have critical roles in helping lead us to that envisioned future.

Organization-making is a never-ending, always evolving, and ongoing task of a leader because of the triangulation process described in the last chapter. You are constantly receiving feedback and learning and listening to your community or customers, and as such, roles emerge, and the composing of the organization shifts along with that understanding.

Tips for Organization Making

At Teleios, after we finish our annual planning for the upcoming year, I take the opportunity to consider how our organization is composed. I look at our meeting structure because, often, meetings are the playground where the team gets to perform together. I knew this needed to be part of our culture through mistakes I made in the past. I learned that I must have the space and freedom to compose the organization without being hindered by politics. What I mean by this is I

Making the Organization

can think of several examples in the past when I knew the organization needed to be composed differently. I would not make changes out of fear that someone's feelings or ego would be harmed. Perhaps someone on the Senior Team or leadership team needed to be changed, given the upcoming challenges of the new year.

From the inception of Teleios, each fall before our next fiscal year, I remind our team that we serve the organization and that part of my role as CEO is to compose the organization so we can fulfill our role descriptions and move forward with our operational plan for the coming year. The mission comes first, and our egos are not at the front of the line of priorities. I will admit it is still hard, but having the latitude to do what is right for the organization has shown in our results.

I have been part of five startups, and one thing I have learned is that composing the organization is critical as the organization's life cycle moves forward. Years ago, I heard Andy Stanley, the pastor of North Point Community Church, say, "Leaders should picture the organizational chart five years from now and even draw it." Today, the team may cover five or six boxes on that organizational chart. However, as the organization continues to evolve, the current leaders' roles evolve, and their role gets deeper and richer in the context of the mission and where the organization is headed. This evolution frees up prior boxes on the organizational chart to recruit new team members to take over parts of the current roles and to go deeper and wider on what the roles entail. This pattern is especially true of younger organizations. As the organization moves forward, periodically composing the organization is necessary to ensure the mission and vision move forward. If you do not continue composing the organization, it will hinder the other M's covered thus far of Mission, Margin, Meaning Management, and Messaging into the Community.

I was thinking recently about when Dr. Thayer said to me, "Do you know what your problem is?" I thought, *No, but I bet you will tell me.* He said, "You are too competent." I remember walking away thinking, *What the heck does that even mean?* Well, I can tell you what it means now. It applies to making the organization and will segue us to the next chapter of people-making. Dr. Thayer meant that if I were overly competent, I would own other people's problems and steal opportunities to learn and grow from them. As a result, the organization would not fulfill its intended destiny, cause, and purpose. How about you? Are there days where you are stealing other people's opportunities to learn and grow? Why do you do that? Jot down your thoughts.

Making the Organization

I can see in the past when I unconsciously prevented leaders in the organization from playing their roles. It gave them permission or frustrated them so much that they did not try to own problems they needed to own based on their role. *I mean, why try if Chris is just going to come in and fix it or do it his way anyway?* Can you see how this negatively impacts a well-composed organization? If my role is the coach and I run on the field, fielding balls for everyone else, it will be hard for the team to perform as intended. Dr. Thayer nailed me, and I remember that lesson even still.

Just like an orchestra's conductor, the composition and utilization of the orchestra produce beautiful music if fully competent. Also, a great conductor does not run down and play the instruments for his team. Instead, a great conductor enables their team to play their best music. How is the music of your organization? How are the moments of truth? How your team is composed has considerable influence on the outcomes.

"As I mentioned, there are several components to our success, it isn't one particular thing we have done, but may be described as everyone, and I mean everyone is playing their instrument in tune, on time, and the same sheet of music. We are an orchestra playing beautiful music."

Suzi Johnson

Questions to Ponder

- Is your current organization composition effective? How would you know? What do your outcomes tell you?
- How did your current structure develop? Was it intentional, or did it just happen?

Making the Organization

- Do you know your team members' superpowers? If not, why not ask them?
- If you optimally composed your organization based on peoples' superpowers while also stretching them where they need to be stretched, how would the new structure look?
- Where are your talent gaps? What are the missing roles? What are the missing skill sets?
- Are there innovative ways you could fill those roles besides recruiting and hiring, especially if your budget will not allow it?
- What is your biggest "Aha" from this chapter? What do you need to do about it?

_____

_____

_____

_____

_____

_____

The Anatomy of Leadership

"In times of change, learners inherit the earth, while the unlearned find themselves beautifully equipped to deal with a world that no longer exists."

Eric Hoffer

Chapter 13: *Making People*

- **Mission**
- **Margin**
- **Meaning Management**
- **Message into the Community**
- **Making the Organization**
- **Making People**
- Mapping the Future

My wife and I have five wonderful kids, but nope, that is not what I mean by people-making. Rather, what I mean draws from two parts of the Anatomy of Leadership shared at the beginning of this book, I based on key fundamentals, including:

Self-Mastery: You cannot lead others if you are not on a journey to be the master of yourself. It is a lifelong journey with no destination, but you must be on the journey. If not, you will not be good for yourself and will not effectively lead others. The journey is about self-mastery, which we referred to earlier in this book.

Caring for Others: You will not let those you are entrusted to lead default themselves. You will provide guidance, challenges, mentoring, coaching, and unconditional love for them to realize their best selves.

People-making draws from caring for others, as you cannot give what you do not have. This is why self-mastery is essential to you, the leader.

Making People Exemplars

To illustrate making people further, a great example in the sports world today is Coach Nick Saban of the University of Alabama. There are hundreds of coaches at the collegiate level that Coach Saban has either impacted because they played for or against him or who have been coaches on his staff. When I was growing up, a similar example was Coach Tom Landry of the Dallas Cowboys. So many coaches who later coached against and after him in the NFL got their start with him. Both men were great people makers, whether it was their players or those coaching with them. Leaders replicate themselves via others. In his book *21 Irrefutable Laws of Leadership*, John Maxwell called it the Law of Replication. I call it people-making, and while replication is in the ballpark, the goal is not to create carbon copies of us, the leader. Instead, it is to help the people around you discover and realize the best version of themselves to set them on their leadership journey, where they will also impact many others. The learning mode is critical to people-making.

Making People Defined

Making people is a leadership philosophy and practice emphasizing the importance of helping team members become the best versions of themselves. It is based on the belief that a leader's primary responsibility is to develop the people under their care. Doing so will lead to better individual, team, and organization outcomes.

At the heart of making people is the idea that people are not objects to be managed but individuals with their own unique strengths, weaknesses, and potential for growth. Your job as a leader is to help your team members identify and leverage their strengths, overcome their weaknesses, and grow into the best versions of themselves.

Making people has several components:

High Expectations: Leaders should set high expectations for team members that are challenging yet achievable and aligned with the team member's strengths and aspirations. By setting high expectations and providing the support and resources needed to meet them, a leader can help their team members achieve their full potential.

Learning from Mistakes: Leaders who embrace people-making understand that people learn best from their mistakes and that failure is a necessary part of the learning process. Create an environment that encourages risk-taking, experimentation, and learning from failure.

Ongoing Feedback and Coaching: Leaders should provide regular feedback to their team members, both positive and constructive, and help them identify areas for improvement and opportunities for growth. They should also provide ongoing coaching and support to help team members develop the skills and knowledge they need to succeed.

Collaboration: People-making is a collaborative process between the leader and the team member. The leader's role is to provide guidance, support, and resources while the team member takes ownership of their own development and growth.

Relationship Building: Leaders committed to people-making must build strong relationships with their team members. They must get to know each individual personally, understand their goals and aspirations and help them align their work with their values and vision.

People-making also depends on a principle we have used several times that must be woven into your organization's culture: the learning mode.

Learning Mode

The learning mode means approaching every day as a new opportunity to gain experience and grow. To approach life with an insatiable curiosity, not as one with all the answers but as one with great questions. Questions are life-giving and thought-provoking, whereas giving answers is not. Providing answers often shuts down learning and growth for you and the person you are leading. Questions are utilized frequently and often to foster a culture and an environment of the learning mode.

> **Acton Academy**
>
> At a recent leadership training at Teleios, we played a video of Acton Academy. https://www.actonacademy.org/. Acton utilizes the Socratic method for their unique school. The teachers do not give answers; they present cases full of learning lessons and start with questions. Their role is to use questions to promote learning. If you watch any videos on YouTube or their website, you will see the learning mode illustrated beautifully. You will also see children blossoming; that is the art of people making in action.

When the Student Is Ready, the Teacher Appears

I first heard this phrase from my mentor, Quint Studer, and have used it many times. Have you ever been in a circumstance where something you may have heard before did not stick? Then you hear it again, and it hits you like lightning. You finally get the lesson, or it sinks in at a much deeper level. That illustrates the phrase *when the student is ready, the teacher appears*. As the leader performing people-making, how do you make it necessary for people to be in the learning mode?

Making People

When Quint presents something important, he has a knack for homing in on the person falling asleep or not paying attention. This must be the schoolteacher in him, but if you accidentally doze off, you could easily find him standing before you asking a question. It only happened to me once, and I remembered it profoundly. That is what leaders do. They care so much about those they are entrusted to lead and want you to succeed as badly as you do.

Dr. Thayer was fond of saying that hanging out with the students in the coffee shop after class was more important to him than the classroom. His students would gather around him and ask him questions. The students were ready, and he loved the banter and asking questions back to them. My experience with him was similar. Some of the most memorable times were outside the classroom, where we would sit over lunch, dinner, or wine and discuss interesting topics. One of our last conversations centered around artificial intelligence. Here was a man late in his life with only about three years left to live, and he was still living life in the learning mode. Based on age, you might not have thought he was informed about technology. He had profound insight into many of the fundamental, challenging questions that artificial intelligence will bring to a head in the next five years.

> *"To the mind that wishes to learn, everything is a lesson."*
>
> **Confucius**

The Lessons of People Making Are All Around If You Look for Them

Recently, I watched the film *Kung Fu Panda 2* with my family. At the movie's beginning, there is a scene where the Panda's sensei catches a raindrop on his hand while doing Tai Chi. He wields it, moves with it, flows with it, and brings the raindrop gently, with fluidity, down to a blade of grass, letting it roll off the tip of his finger. Finally, the blade of grass ever-so-lightly bends, and the raindrop rolls off and is absorbed into the water of a pond.

Unfortunately, while awed by the demonstration, the Panda does not seem to be learning and growing from the tutelage of his sensei. The people-making does not seem to be working. Hopefully, this is not a spoiler if you have not seen the movie, but finally, the lessons seem to stick after a series of major setbacks and then fast-forward to the movie's end. The Panda, who has failed often but who has constantly been in the learning mode, catches a cannonball, wields it, moves with it (mind you, it is a cannonball fired at him), absorbs its energy, redirects its energy, and then throws it back at the firing cannon. What a great visual of the fruits of people-making. The movie is also a great illustration of when the student is ready, the teacher appears, and there is nothing more rewarding than for the student to surpass the teacher.

Making people depends on growing yourself, being in the learning mode, and ensuring that all within your organization are on that same journey. Not because you demand it of them but because there is no better way to transform your life and their lives and help to make them better people.

In his book *The Energy Bus*, Jon Gordon includes ten rules for the ride of your life. One of these critical rules is to love your passengers. Do you love your passengers? If an impartial observer asked your team, what would your team tell them? Jot down some notes.

_____

_____

_____

_____

_____

Mentors in Our Life Who Performed People-Making with Us

Can you think of a time in your career when a teacher, coach, professor, parent, or family member brought out the best in you? And they did it not by patting you on the head but by challenging you in such a way that brought out a talent in you that you did not know existed? If you are so fortunate, think back to that person. At the core level, did you know they wanted the best for you and, at some level, loved you and wanted more for you than you ever wanted for yourself? Congratulations! If you can answer yes to these questions, consider writing that person(s) a thank you note. Now, how can you be that type of leader for those you have been entrusted to lead?

As I shared in Chapter 2, Mrs. Wyble was that type of teacher for me and my classmates. She brought out skills, talents, and possibilities in us that we did not know were there. That is what people-making does.

My high school football coach was also a great mentor. To this day, I use one of his great lessons about football. His name was Coach Nagata, and he was a Japanese American. If you know history, then you know that during World War II, Japanese Americans were put into internment camps here in the United States because of mistrust of

Making People

anyone of Japanese descent after the attack on Pearl Harbor. Coach Nagata's family was put into one of those camps while he went to war to fight for the United States.

Can you imagine the racism he encountered? Yet he went on to be a decorated war hero. I share this because it tells you what kind of man he was, and he was a great people-maker. He would often say the game of football was not that complicated. Get a helmet on the other guy and get the football in the hands of one of the most talented people on the field, and you will score a touchdown every time. To this day, I use this analogy: *let's get a helmet on it* with our team regarding the challenges headed our way, at least the ones we know about. Coach Nagata was a great people-maker, and here I am, paying that lesson forward to hundreds of people almost forty years later. That is what people makers do.

Ultimately, making people is about creating a culture of growth, learning, and continuous improvement. Leaders who embrace this philosophy are committed to helping their team members become the best version of themselves, and in doing so, they create more engaged, productive, and successful teams.

Tactics in People-Making

Here are tactics that we have found at Teleios that help create a culture of people-making:

- Use the Socratic method in day-to-day interactions. Ask more questions and give fewer instructions.
- Hunt the status quo like it is the enemy. Do not allow cliches to rule conversations. Push back, ask questions, and promote real understanding. Keep people on their toes and challenge them to bring their A-game every day.
- Provide leadership training on a frequent and ongoing basis. Many of our Teleios member organizations create Leadership Development Institutes or Leadership Training series where they intentionally use material that furthers the learning and growth of all involved. Team members are encouraged to engage in this training.
- Use learning plans. As shared earlier and in Appendix 1, codifying a tool like a learning plan makes learning necessary and expected for all your team members.

Making People

"Leadership is a potent combination of strategy and character. But if you must be without one, be without the strategy."

General Norman H. Schwarzkopf

Questions to Ponder

- How can you apply people-making principles to your leadership style and practice?
- What specific actions can you take to help your team members become the best version of themselves?
- How can you create a culture of growth and learning within your team or organization?
- How can you foster a collaborative relationship with your team members, where they take ownership of their development and growth?
- How can you set high expectations for your team members while providing the support and resources needed to meet those expectations?
- How can you create an environment that encourages risk-taking,

experimentation, and learning from failure?

- How can you provide ongoing feedback and coaching to your team members to help them develop the skills and knowledge they need to succeed?

"Creators start at the end. First, they have an idea of what they want to create. Sometimes this idea is general, and sometimes it is specific. Before you can create what you want to create, you must know what you are after, what you want to bring into being."

Robert Fritz

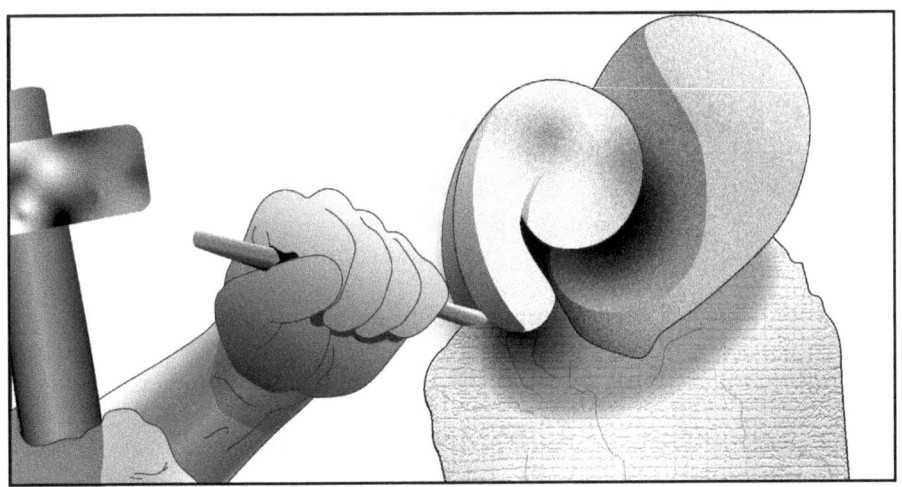

Chapter 14: *Mapping the Future*

- **Mission**
- **Margin**
- **Meaning Management**
- **Message into the Community**
- **Making the organization**
- **Making people**
- **Mapping the Future**

How does your organization know if it is on track if it has no idea where it is going? Mapping the future is about charting a course for your organization. At Teleios, we have many tools our members use to help map their future.

First Is a Vision Statement

As we travel through life, it is tempting just to allow life to happen to us—why not? Life is unpredictable, and some of the sweetest moments in life are spontaneous and unplanned. Sometimes, those moments become defining moments, propelling us forward, helping us realize our blessings come from outside of ourselves, and checking our pulse when it comes to what we think we can control.

However, leaving everything to chance can rob us of even greater blessings. Lacking vision is much like steering a ship without a rudder. We may eventually arrive at a destination, but was it the one we desired?

Several years ago, my family and I drove from North Carolina to Yellowstone National Park. We meticulously planned every detail of the two-week trip. We talked about it constantly in the days leading up to our departure. All the planning and anticipation created the vision and hope for what the trip would be like.

The trip was incredible, and each family member will carry memories of that vacation for the rest of our lives. However, not everything about the trip went as planned. In fact, one of the best memories we made was in an Old West replica town that was not even on our agenda. And one of the biggest disappointments of the trip was something we *planned to a T* and drove out of our way to see.

Life is like that. Things will not always go as planned, which is a good thing. If we had left for our trip with no plans or expectations, we would have had no picture in our minds of the dream that could be.

A Vision Statement is much like an exciting trip agenda—it calls us and our teams forward, giving us hope and an image of what could be. Often, the gestalt of the reality of the journey is even better than we imagined.

It Is Not What the Vision Is; It Is What the Vision Does

The title of this section is one of my favorite quotes from Peter Senge. He wrote about how the secret sauce of a vision statement is not necessarily what it says but rather what it does in terms of calling you forth on the journey.

The Anatomy of Leadership

While working for the Studer group, I got invited back for the ribbon cutting to open the expansion of Four Seasons' Hospice House, the Elizabeth House. On the plane ride over, I had just finished Peter Senge's book, *The 5th Discipline*, and that phrase: *it is not what the vision is, it is what the vision does*, stuck with me. I utilized it in my speech for the ribbon cutting and dedication ceremony to re-open the Elizabeth House.

Consider they were about to open a home where thousands of people would spend their last days with family members surrounding them, reflecting upon their lives. To expand the size of the Elizabeth House was the product of a miraculous fundraising venture that ended up being the largest ever capital campaign at the time in the county's history. Senge's phrase was a fitting way to remind us of the vision of expanding this much-needed facility while simultaneously pushing everyone's gaze to the horizon of all the incredible stories still to come in this special place.

It is not what the vision is; it is what the vision does. Great visions and great vision statements are like that. It is not about the vision or the statement but the journey we are driven to take. That is what mapping the future is all about.

Notable Examples of Vision Statements of Well-Known Organizations

- **Amazon:** "Our vision is to be earth's most customer-centric company, where customers can find and discover anything they might want to buy online."

- **Avon:** "To be the company that best understands and satisfies the product, service, and self-fulfillment needs of women—globally."

- **Ford:** "People working together as a lean, global enterprise to make people's lives better through automotive and mobility leadership."

- **IBM:** "To be the world's most successful and important information technology company. Successful in helping our customers apply technology to solve their problems. Successful in introducing this extraordinary technology to new customers. Important because we will continue to be the basic resource of much of what is invested in this industry."

- **McDonald's:** "To move with velocity to drive profitable growth and become an even better McDonald's serving more customers delicious food each day around the world."

- **Nordstrom:** "To serve our customers better, to always be relevant in their lives, and to form lifelong relationships."

- **Starbucks:** "To establish Starbucks as the premier purveyor of the finest coffee in the world while maintaining our uncompromising principles while we grow."

Strategic Planning

After you have a vision of where you and your team want to go, you must develop a plan of how you will get there. We learned the core of the strategic planning process we utilize at Teleios from Meridith Elliott Powell, a dynamic leader, speaker, and author. She speaks internationally, and we were blessed to have her on our Board at Four Seasons before Teleios was founded. She taught us her process, and we refined it to what it is today. If you do research, there are two general schools of thought on strategic planning. One view is the future is too uncertain, so why even plan? The other, which we subscribe to, is that the best way to predict the future is to create it. But we also know that the future has lots of challenges. If you research the general macro trends, you can plot a general course for the next ten years, a more specific course for the next three years, and then a specific one-year operational plan aligned with the three-year plan. On the next page is an illustration of our process.

One way to think about mapping is if you have ever driven on a dark night. Your headlights illuminate out as far as they can, about 350 feet or so, and while you can see to that extent, it is most clear right in front of you, a little less clear farther out, and so forth. This wisdom is

Mapping the Future

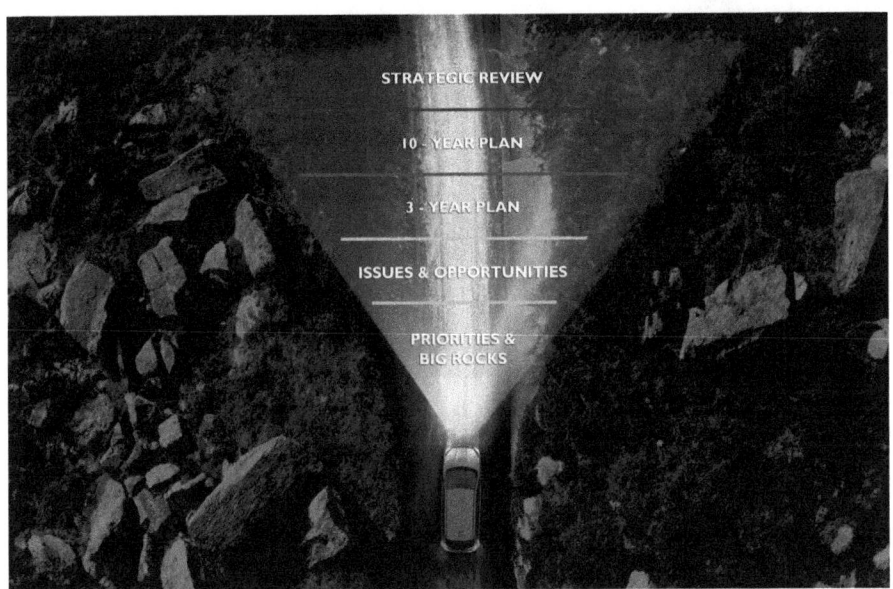

what we are utilizing in our strategic planning process. While not as clear, your ten-year plan is documented via the general sense of where you intend to be. Creating this plan gives you time to think about pictures and visions. You are tapping the right side of your brain, the more creative side. Then, you bring it down more to a three-year plan with quantitative measures showing you are moving toward those visions for the ten-year plan. You are tapping the right and left sides of your brain, the analytical and creative brains.

A Bill Gates quote applies here: "People overestimate what they can accomplish in five years and underestimate what they can accomplish in ten." This approach honors that wisdom.

The One-Year Operational Plan

Where the rubber meets the road in this planning process and mapping process is the one-year operational plan, which is organized by a concept known as Pillars.

Often, I ask people, "What do you think of when you hear the word Pillars?" Usually, people refer to pillars that hold up a house, which is a great visual. Our visual here depicts that.

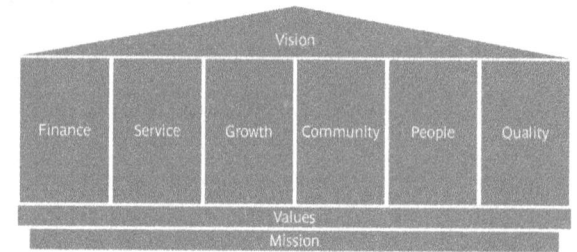

But our visual also shows the house divided into segments, illustrating the wisdom often lost.

Wisdom Gleaned from Hospice

To digress for a short trip, do you know what makes hospice care special and different? Most folks who have been around it for as long

Mapping the Future

as I have, going on twenty-eight-plus years, will say it is care that takes a complex human and breaks them into these categories: body, mind, spirit, and a social-emotional component. The categories allow you to take a complex system and break it into components that are all interrelated, helping everyone think about the complex system methodically. Great clinicians do this naturally, realizing one part affects another part. But let me speak to the businesspeople as well. Have you ever heard of a balanced scorecard? In the late 1980s and 1990s, this wisdom caught on to look at an organization's financial aspect and other aspects like service, quality, culture, people, etc.

Have you had your physical recently? Did you sit with the doctor as they went over your various lab results? There was a lot there, right? If you have a good provider, they help you understand how one part of your results affects another. That is systemic thinking. Leaders who go through operational planning for the first time come away enlightened because they think about their organization in holistic ways that they have not before. Pillars help you look at your organization holistically and systemically.

"Whether as an army, a nation, or a corporation - people become unstoppable when they are moved by a common vision and have the power and tools to achieve it."

United Technologies Corporation

Utilizing Pillars for your One-Year Plan

Typically, we will start with the pillars depicted here: Finance, Service and Quality, Growth, Community, and People. Once we are further on the journey, we help organizations develop Pillars that are unique to their organization and align with their ten-year and three-year

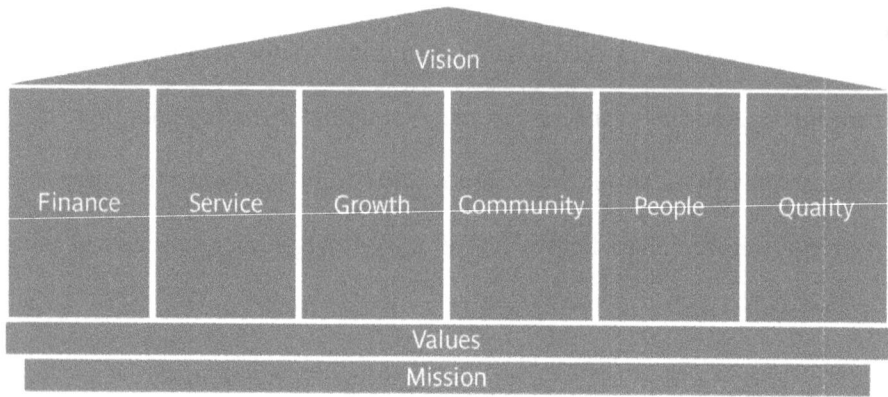

strategic plans.

We have a specific format for the one-year operational plan, depicted in Appendix 3. We start each pillar with a BHAG, which comes from Jim Collins and is the big, hairy, audacious goal for the Pillar. It serves two purposes. First, the BHAG calls your organization forward towards the vision and defines that pillar. Then, the pillar has goals but goals that are specific, measurable, action-oriented, realistic, and time-bound. Lastly, under the goal, we identify action plans of how we will accomplish the goal with clear accountabilities of who will be owning or working on that action plan. Also, to create a rhythm and cadence for our year, we lay out which quarter we anticipate working on that action plan.

One of the many brilliant aspects of hospice care is a care plan, as it can ensure the team members working on someone's care are pulling in the same direction. Similarly, the One-Year Operational Plan has that potential for a team and an organization.

The Challenges We Might Face on The Journey

Backing up a little bit to know where you are headed, you also need to be prepared for the terrain and challenges you may encounter. To know where you are headed, you must have a good assessment of the external environment, where things currently are, and some prediction of where things are headed. As part of this assessment, you need to reconnect with who your community or customers are and their current and future needs. You can then identify the intersection of where things are headed and those needs. Understanding the needs aligns with the M of messaging into the community. You will then need a good internal assessment of your organization's readiness to navigate the predicted future. It is always good at this point to check the mapping to ensure that it aligns with your Mission, Vision, and Values. As an organization, your Mission, Vision, and Values serve as your compass to help you navigate the journey you want to undertake.

Many organizations use a simple SWOT analysis when assessing the items above. However, in my experience, SWOT analyses are more internally focused when you need both an external reading and an internal readiness assessment. At Teleios, we utilize the system we learned from Meridith called Future External Environmental Scan (FEES). This tool takes the Opportunities and Threats of a SWOT and gives you a much more robust way to look at the external world via an acronym called SKEPTIC: Society, Competition, Economics, Political/Regulatory, Technology, Industry, and Customers. Using this tool, we identify the macro trends we will encounter over the next ten years. We frequently revisit and update this list. It results in a document called *The Challenges We Will Face*.

Then, for an internal assessment, which is usually the Strengths and Weaknesses of the SWOT, we utilize Meridith's Seeds, Weeds, and Needs. This tool challenges you to identify the seeds in your organization that need to be watered and cultivated, what weeds are hampering our progress and need to be eliminated, and the needs or gaps in our organization, given the opportunities and challenges we see ahead.

Prow of the Ship

Finally, at Teleios, we have developed a tool to help us as we navigate this mapping of the future. It is called the Prow of the Ship Questions.

The background on Prow of the Ship is when I was working on my master's in leadership. Dr. Thayer chastised our class as leaders, telling us we spent too much time looking at the ship's wake. While financials, satisfaction survey scores, and quality scores are important, they are the wake of the ship. In other words, our actions that created those outcomes are now far behind us. So very slowly, almost timidly, I raised my hand and asked, "What would be the things we would be asking if we were looking off the prow of the ship?" His answer blew me away, and I furiously took notes. Those questions have been refined and re-refined into what has now become the Prow of the Ship Questions. Thinking about these and identifying answers builds the muscle of navigating your organization based on your mapping.

To align this with meaning management, the better a team gets at answering the Prow of the Ship Questions, the more they build the competency to identify need to know communication as they encounter it in their roles throughout the week.

Let's review the Prow of the Ship Questions. Keep these in mind each day as you perform your role to help build the muscle of identifying what is need to know and what to do with it once you have identified it. I have used the phrase *need to know* throughout the book and have waited until now to define it because it will make the most sense in the context of the Prow of the Ship questions. *Need to know*, or *NTK*, as we refer to it at Teleios, means harvesting what you need to know from others and interactions in as few words as possible, predicated upon your role description. It also means paying forward NTK in as few words as possible what others need to know to perform their roles. To illustrate further, do you remember *The Ghost in the Darkness* movie metaphor in Chapter 11? It is a great metaphor for a team looking out into the world with a 360-degree view harvesting the NTK. The Prow of the Ship Questions are questions that while one leader alone may not know the answer to all these questions, the full complement of the leadership team's collective wisdom looking out into the world will have the answer to these questions in their heads if they are in learning mode. Contemplating questions as a team is a way to collect the answers and train leaders to pay forward critical need to know information.

So, let's jump into the Prow of the Ship Questions.

Prow of the Ship Questions

1. What is the organization's performance if you can only measure this in the eyes, minds, and hearts of those who use your services? What is our performance via "the moments of truth" today?

2. What are the numbers and trends or indicators of things in the environment that affect our performance, purpose, and cause?

   What we mean by environment are external factors. For example, in hospice, how many people are becoming Medicare eligible daily, the number of deaths by county, substitution competition. etc. Do we know the answer to this question? As an aside, Teleios has some incredible tools to enable any team or organization to do a Competitive Strength Analysis (CSA) of the main competitors in your area and or anticipated competitors. Those CSA tools help build muscle and provide the need to know to answer this question.

3. Do we have any problems or potential problems that may impact the performance of this organization? Do we have service recoveries? Do we have vulnerable areas or departments in our organization, and do we know this through the number of errors occurring in that area?

4. We want to know about new people coming in and going out; this is a great predictor of the organization's future performance. Ask

yourself, are we hiring rock stars and losing dead wood? Or is it the opposite, we are hiring dead wood and losing rock stars?

If it is the latter, then you can predict where the organization's performance will be six months to a year from now. This question is one of the most significant predictors of our future. Teams often say, "We are concerned about turnover." I usually share this question with them and even ask them to rate this on a ten-point scale. Ten means we are hiring the rock stars and losing the deadwood, and one means we are losing the rock stars and hiring the deadwood. How about your team, organization, or department? How would you rate them for this question? And given your answer, you now have need to know you should pay forward.

5. As you look out from the prow of the ship, what opportunities do you see? What new lands do you see where we can explore and create a new future?

This is a fun question. When you and your team train, read or attend conferences, do you see opportunities for your organization? Think about your last training. Did it generate ideas for you? Did you pay that need to know forward to anyone? They say everyone gets the idea in the shower. What separates high performers is they do something with that idea when they get out of the shower.

6. Communication is the lubricant, the mode, and the medium of all interactions. The meaning of things is communication, and communication creates the meaning of things. How are we doing in this area? Think about this for your team, department, or organization. Rate this with ten being the best and one being the worst.

7. What is the spirit of the place? How is it rumbling? What is the aura, spirit, or soul of the place? Think about that for a moment. What is your answer? Given your answer, is there someone you should share this information with, and would it be need to know for them?

8. This question focuses on our cause and purpose. What is the overall state of our purpose and our cause—is it healthy or unhealthy? This is a gestalt question. This means that given the preponderance of other questions, what is the state of our cause and purpose? Think about

that now for your organization and your team or department. How would you rank it, with ten being the best and one being the worst?

The Anatomy of Leadership

You can see how difficult it is to find the time to utilize all these tools to map the future, but with them, it is possible, and all the other M's help aid in mapping the future as well.

"Impossible is just a big word thrown around by small men who find it easier to live in a world they've been given than to explore the power they have to change it."

Adidas

Questions to Ponder

- How can you use mapping the future to align your organization's mission, vision, and values with its long-term goals and objectives?
- How can you use scenario planning and other techniques to anticipate and prepare for potential future trends and disruptions?
- How can you ensure that your mapping of the future is flexible and adaptable to changing market conditions, customer needs, and emerging technologies?
- How can you ensure that your strategic plan (i.e., the result of mapping the future) is integrated into your day-to-day operations and decision-making processes?

- How can you develop a process for regularly reviewing and updating your strategic plan to ensure it remains relevant and effective over time?

Conclusion

What leadership is and the 7 M's of Leadership, which is what leaders do

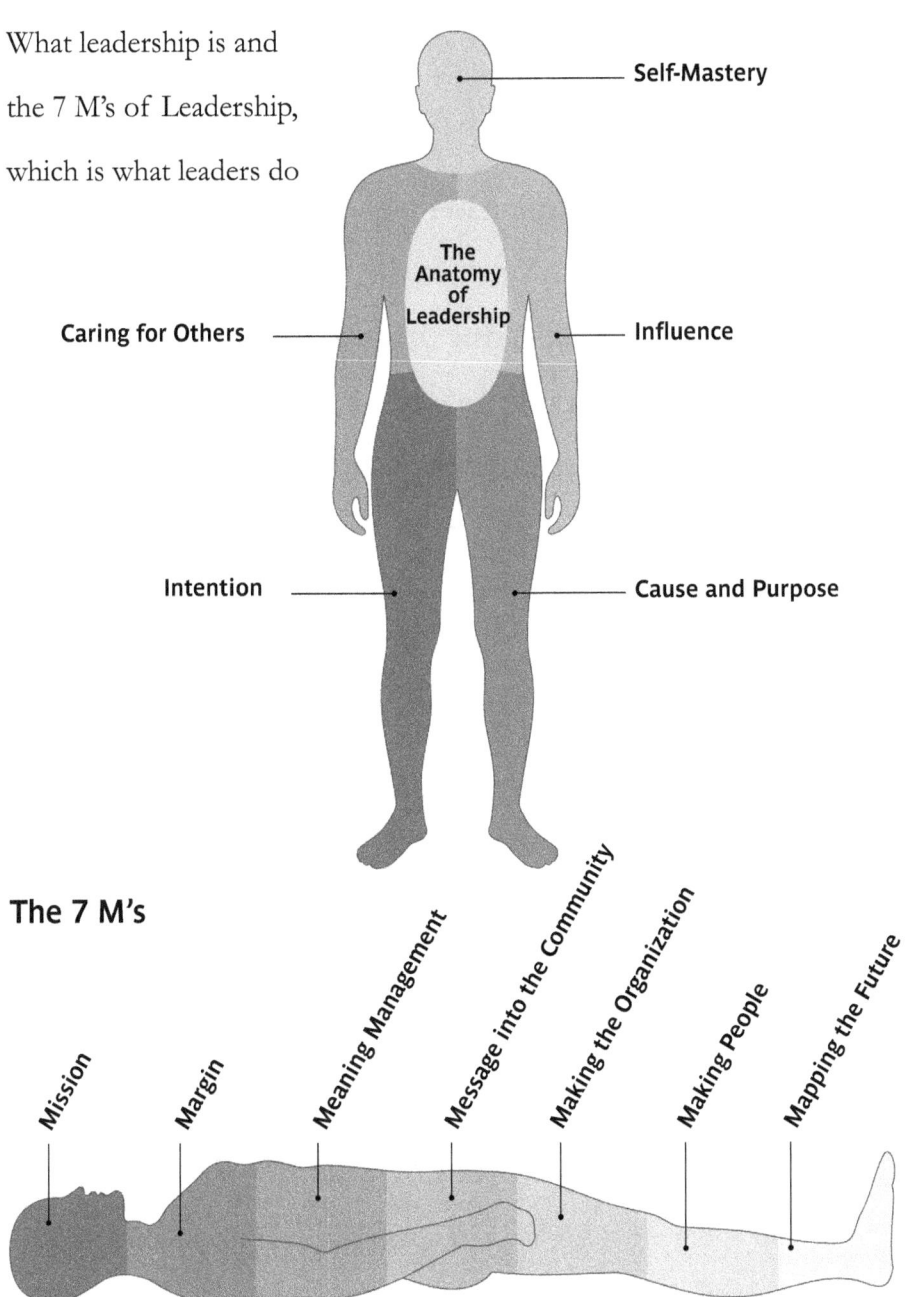

- Self-Mastery
- Caring for Others
- The Anatomy of Leadership
- Influence
- Intention
- Cause and Purpose

The 7 M's

- Mission
- Margin
- Meaning Management
- Message into the Community
- Making the Organization
- Making People
- Mapping the Future

- **Mission**
- **Margin**
- **Meaning Management**
- **Message into the Community**
- **Making the organization**
- **Making people**
- **Mapping the Future**

So, there you have it, the 7 M's of being a leader: Mission, Margin, Meaning Management, Message into the Community, Making the Organization, Making People, and Mapping the Future. These competencies of what leaders do may take you a lifetime to master. However, creating a high-performance organization, which can only be called that if it is made up of high-performing people, is well worth the journey because, in the process, you will become better yourself, and so will those around you.

You Cannot Get the Fruits Without the Roots

While shopping at Lowe's, I was reflecting on how to conclude this book and noticed something I had looked over many times before. I was

Conclusion

shopping for blueberry and raspberry bushes for our farm. Have you ever noticed the tags on the bushes depicting the fruit growing on the tree? It is brilliant marketing. The tags give you a vision of what the bush  can be if the soil, cultivation, pruning, and overall care are suitable. If all we saw was the planting and hard work without getting a vision for the fruits, I am not sure we would buy the plant.

I often think I forget to paint the picture of the fruits of the journey of leadership and mastering the 7 M's. I get so excited about the hard work and teaching people the tools, but I forget that I am already bought in because I have seen the fruits, and at Teleios, we see the fruits with our members. The Anatomy of Leadership and the 7 M's are essential to establishing the roots that bring forth both personal and organizational fruit that is lasting and sweet. It is hard work to get there, but the fruits are sweet indeed. What are they?

- Happy people
- Better outcomes
- Learning every day
- Beautiful moments of truth

As Dr. Thayer said, "Bringing life back into the performance of every role and hence daily life itself."

"Success is not final, failure is not fatal: It is the courage to continue that counts."

Winston Churchill

Symbols Of Leadership That Tie the Anatomy All Together

I have one last thought to push your thinking regarding leadership. I was recently reminded of the importance of symbols because they use pictures to teach us what words cannot always achieve. As I pondered their importance, two specific symbols about leadership and the significant lessons they have taught me immediately came to mind.

During my Master's in Leadership program with Dr. Lee Thayer many years ago, he taught us that one of the commonly used Chinese symbols for leadership represented someone whose feet are planted firmly on the ground while reaching for the stars.

Conclusion

What do you make of that symbol? I believe it teaches us two important truths about leadership that are seemingly opposed but are meant to work in concert and harmony:

Mapping the Future: Consider reaching for the stars—it seems like the easy part, right? It is vision-casting, reaching toward the future, and doing something that has never been done. In many ways, it is the sexy part of leadership.

Honest Assessment: The ability to take stock of what pieces you have to make the dream come true is often forgotten or cast aside into the shadows. It is not as fun as mapping the future.

As John Maxwell says, "Every dream is built upon the foundation of reality." Without a foot on the ground, we'd float among the stars with no real ability to achieve anything. To accomplish something, we must take an honest look at where we are—our team, our department, our organization—start building from there and then do the work. Deluding ourselves by focusing only on the stars is foolhardy; our dreams must be built upon the foundation of reality, and we must do the work.

The Anatomy of Leadership and the 7 M's are my attempts to give you the necessary tools, turning your visions and your dreams into reality, hence living your cause and purpose.

The Anatomy of Leadership

Permit me one final analogy. On many occasions, speaking on leadership, I have utilized the *vision of the eagle*. Did you know when an eagle flies, it can see in two directions at once? Eagles can view the horizon and simultaneously look down for their food. I believe this is such a significant metaphor for leadership. Similar to the Chinese leadership symbol, it represents the importance of looking at where you are going while also looking at the proverbial *ground*—the day-to-day, the most current needs, and the current reality.

One of the most important tools I teach as part of our Teleios Leadership System is *The 7 Fundamentals Of Every Organization System.*

A central premise of the fundamentals is that you can have the vision and work towards it, but if you do not have the tools to do it daily, it is simply a pipe dream. This will be the subject of my next book to continue giving you the tools to live your cause and purpose.

The 7 Fundamentals Of Every Organization System

- Calendar
- Task List
- Intake System
- Reference System
- Contacts
- Daily/Weekly Review
- Cause and Purpose

Conclusion

What is the overarching learning lesson in all this symbology? Each of these symbols represents the obvious yin and yang of leadership. Most of us come into our leadership journey with a proclivity for one or the other, but the rarified air is a leader who can do both. The journey of leadership learning is mastery on both continuums.

Based on all we have learned thus far, are you a high-performing leader? Is your organization a high-performing organization?

Rate yourself in the 7 M's of a leader on a scale of 1 to 10, with 10 being masterful and 1 being awful. Give it a try; honestly assess yourself. Now, rate your organization. How well does your organization perform in these areas?

7 M's Category	1 - 10 Your Rating	1 - 10 Your Organization's Rating
Mission	_____	_____
Margin	_____	_____
Meaning Management	_____	_____
Message into the Community	_____	_____
Making the Organization	_____	_____
Making People	_____	_____
Mapping the Future	_____	_____

Create or edit your learning plan based on what you learn from this exercise (Appendix 1). What "Aha's!" did you have as you read each chapter covering the 7 M's above? Codify those in your learning plan.

If we embody or exemplify the 7 M's of leadership (Mission, Margin, Meaning Management, Message into the Community, Making the organization, Making people, and Mapping the Future) I believe that in the future when someone asks, "Who were the leaders of the 21st Century?" the answer would be that there were too many to count because they embodied the contents of this book and set out to change a team, a department, an organization, a family, or a community.

"I am afraid of an army of one hundred sheep led by a lion than an army of one hundred lions led by a sheep."

Charles, Count Talleyrand

Given our definition of The Anatomy of Leadership and the 7 M's, are you a high-performance leader?

Conclusion

Now that you know what leadership is via The Anatomy of Leadership, is there anything you think I missed in that definition?

_____

_____

_____

_____

_____

_____

The 7 M's gives you a framework for a leader's role. Is there anything you think I missed in the 7 M's? Please send your thoughts to ccomeaux@teleioscn.org. I would love to hear from you and will gladly pay you $100 for any principles you offer that add to The Anatomy or the 7 M's.

_____

_____

The Anatomy of Leadership

_____

_____

_____

_____

_____

The learning mode comes from a place of humility. I am still learning every day as I practice leadership. The statement I made in the first paragraph of this chapter bears repeating: The competencies of leadership may take you a lifetime to master, but creating a high-performing organization, which can only be called that if it is made up of high-performing people, is well worth the journey. In the process, you will become better yourself, and so will those around you. Enjoy the journey!

_____

"We do not grow by knowing all the answers, but rather by living with the questions."

Max Depree

From Beginning to the End

At the beginning of the book, I challenged you to jot down some thoughts before you jumped into the book. I asked why you were reading this book and what you hoped to get from it. If you read books without purpose, who knows what you might get? Remember, my purpose in writing this book was to give you a common lexicon or definition of the Anatomy of Leadership and a set of tools for what leaders do, a meta-framework of leadership. Now, revisit your thoughts. Did you accomplish your goal with your reading? How are you different after reading this book? I love the premise that we are changed by the people we meet in this life and by the books we read. Has this book impacted you? If so, how?

_____

_____

_____

_____

_____

_____

Appendix 1: Learning Plan Example

Download a copy of the Learning Plan:

https://teleioscg.com/anatomy-of-leadership

LEARNING PLAN

Name: _____ Date: _____

Strengths in my current role (Where am I now?)

Areas in which I'd like to grow/gain competency (skills, knowledge and behaviors) (Where do I want to go?)

Goal 1: Related to your current role

Objective	Actions	Due Date	Notes

Goal 1: Related to your current role

Objective	Actions	Due Date	Notes

Goal 1: Related to your current role

Objective	Actions	Due Date	Notes

Appendix 2: Role Description Example

Teleios CEO Role Description
Role Summary

Your role is to be the *conductor of the orchestra* for all TCN's activities.

Your role is to be the *chief recruiter* and *organization composer* to build and develop a team (people-making) and to ensure their competence to provide value-added products/solutions, support services, and subject matter specialist coaching for Serious Illness Care.

Your role is to be the TCN *culture cultivator*, ensuring TCN's culture is fluid and dynamic to accomplish our vision, plan, and mission.

Your role is to be the *chief steward of our budget and balance sheet* to ensure our mission and vision continue far into the future in accordance with our ops plan and strategic plan.

Your role is to be the *chief strategy practitioner* who helps uncomplexify our vision and plans to ensure they are dreamed, vetted, and either moved forward or discarded (with learning).

Your role is to be the TCN *organization plan architect, organizer, and provoker.*

Your role is to *coach the TCN team and our TCN Executive* members where needed.

Your role is to be the *chief leadership system virtuoso* learning, implementing, architecting, improving, and capturing via KMR to accelerate TCN and our members' journey.

Your role is to be the *R&D scientist* in the lab developing prototypes related to processes and ideas that will further TCN's mission, operating plan, and strategic plan. The role is to hand the prototype off to the team and let them move it towards perfection.

Summary

Your role is to ensure TCN is the industry leader in discovering and disseminating best practices as well as enabling our partners to implement them operationally as well as achieving clinical integration. Your role is to ensure other hospices are attracted to and discerningly invited to join TCN to cover the US. Your role is to advise and influence the CEOs of the TCN member organizations to ensure their organizations are accomplishing their respective missions and visions, their strategic plans, and their one-year operational plans.

Appendix 3: Operational Plan Example

Download a copy of the Operational Plan:

https://teleioscg.com/anatomy-of-leadership

Pillar BHAG (Big Hairy Audacious Goal)	Action Plan Details	Champion	Action Plan Owner	Quarter Start	Notes
1. Finance					
2. Service					
3. Growth					
5. Community					
6. People					
7. Quality					

Acknowledgments

There are so many to thank in the writing of this book. I am reminded of the adage that two things in this world change us: the books we have read and the people we have met. This is incredibly true for my life. I have been an avid reader since my youth, and I am grateful that my parents instilled a love of books in me at an early age. They sacrificed much for my sisters and me over the years, including investing in us via our education. It is unbelievable that my parents paid more for me to attend elementary and high school than my college tuition at Louisiana State University. Thanks, Mom and Dad; this book would not have been possible without you.

As I mentioned in the dedication, my father-in-law Gerald Eady encouraged and inspired me to write a book. Having a fan in your father-in-law is a blessing. Since Deshia and I have been married, he has consistently asked me when I will write a book. He also asks me about when I am going to run for President. He is the life of any conversation, and spending time with him is a party, the fun family kind. While some might dismiss his prodding as playful teasing, he has always been serious about me writing something to offer to the world one day. So here it is, Pop; thanks for your encouragement. I think I may have several more books in me as well. Thanks for being such a great encourager. I love you very much.

There are so many who, unbeknownst to them, initiated this book via a thought, a question, or a prod. To Jon Wood for performing an assessment of Four Seasons many years ago and telling me news I did not want to hear. You told me that our organization did not have a common definition of leadership. That honesty became the catalyst that resulted in this book.

To Jannelle McCallum, Teleios Chief Clinical Operations Officer, you mused that there were 3M's. This analogy stuck in my brain and got me thinking, reading, researching, and finally concluding that there are seven. However, your three were the catalyst. And to the entire team at Teleios, each of you makes me better every day as we live the learning mode utilizing our lexicon and tools. It is a wonderful learning laboratory, and I could not think of a better team to work with on this learning journey. Also, to our Teleios member organizations, your dedication to learning and growth, and even more importantly, your respective missions, is an inspiration. I pray this book is an accelerant to you and your team's journeys.

Acknowledgments

I was oblivious to the process of making a book, and many people helped with the hard work of bringing this book to life.

To Julie Oehlert Kennedy, thank you for the late evening conversation while I was at the airport and you were driving to Wisconsin. You reviewed the first draft and gave me the most incredible advice, much of which shaped the final product. However, the most important gift you gave me was when you said, "Chris, go back and put your whole heart into this." I pray this hits the mark, as I know I upped my writing game considerably after that conversation. Thanks for challenging me.

Dr. Marie Jones, Professor at Brevard College, thank you for your early encouragement. You invited me to lecture to your class on leadership and followed it up with a review of the early manuscript. You gave wonderful feedback and a pearl of encouragement with the comment, "There are some concepts here on leadership that are fresh and new." Many thanks for affirming what every writer longs to hear: that I might have something worth saying that could impact others. I pray it hits the mark.

To Andie Robbins, you have been a great editor of many of my past blogs, some of which were the jumping-off point for chapters in this book. Please know that your work has a beachhead in this book. To

Dawn Landry for encouraging me after writing your own book and for introducing me to Rana Severs, who has been a great editing partner and publisher for this book. And Rana, thank you. The book would not have come out the way it has without your craft and skill. Thanks to you, I think I am catching on to this writing thing.

To Mark Cohen, you are a virtuosic writer and grammar professional. I enjoy our "Top News Stories of the Month," podcasts in *TCN Talks*. Your question at my first presentation on *The Anatomy of Leadership* was a great thought prodder and your review of the early chapters helped tighten up the editing that followed. Thanks for making me better.

And lastly, to my beautiful wife, Deshia, thank you for supporting me in all my endeavors over our twenty-eight-plus years together. You are my best friend and the best life partner and completer I could have imagined. I love you so much, and thanks again for being the wind beneath my wings. And to our kids: Ian, Gage, Declan, Ava, and Evangeline, you are our best work, and we are so proud of each of you. I cannot wait to see the great good you do with your purposes. I love you very much.

Thank you, Lord, for the many blessings. I press on towards the goal. Much to be done still.

Bibliography

Thayer, Lee. *Leadership: Thinking, Being, Doing.* United States, WME Books, 2007.

Hesselbein, Frances, et al. *The Leader of the Future,* (Drucker FoundationFuture Series): New Visions, Strategies and Practices for the Next Era. Oman, Wiley, 1996.

Bailey, Thomas D. Papers (photocopies). United States, n.p, 1951.

Maxwell, John C. *The 21 Irrefutable Laws of Leadership Workbook : Follow Them and People Will Follow You.* Nashville, Tenn.: Thomas Nelson, 2007.

Webster, Noah. *An American Dictionary of the English Language*: United States, S. Converse, 1828.

Cronin, A. J. "Turning Point of My Career," *Reader's Digest*, 38 (May 1941): 53–57.

Frost, Robert. "The Road Not Taken, A Group of Poems." *The Atlantic Monthly*, August, 1915.

"The Four Steps to Achievement - Plan purposefully. Prepare prayerfully. Proceed positively. Pursue persistently." From the writings of. William Arthur Ward. (1921-1994).

Black, Clint. "Wherever You Go." One Emotion, RCA Records, 1994. Spotify. https://open.spotify.com/track/2ImISB39Tmontq9OIKYe6n.

MBS, Inc. Management By Strengths. From the wisdom of Hippocrates' The Four Basic Temperaments. https://strengths.com/

The John Maxwell Company. https://corporatesolutions.johnmaxwell.com/

Littauer, Florence. *Personality Plus.* India, Manjul Publishing House Pvt Limited, 2008.

CliftonStrengths®. https://www.gallup.com/cliftonstrengths/en/home.aspx.

Coursera. https://www.coursera.org/

"Claritin Clear." https://www.claritin.com/products/claritin.

Collins, James Charles, and Collins, Jim. *Good to Great: Why Some Companies Make the Leap ... and Others Don't*. United Kingdom, Random House Business, 2001.

"Your beliefs become your thoughts..." From the writings of Mahatma Gandhi (1869-1948).

Fritz, Robert. T*he Path of Least Resistance: Learning to Become the Creative Force in Your Own Life*. United Kingdom, Elsevier Science, 2014.

Sharma, Robin. *The 5AM Club: Own Your Morning. Elevate Your Life*. United States, HarperCollins Canada, 2018.

Huberman, Dr. Andrew, host. "Tony Hawk: Harnessing Passion, Drive & Persistence for Lifelong Success" The Huberman Lab Podcast. July 31, 2023. Scicomm Media LLC. https://open.spotify.com/episode/3XnFyRjtNUJKwtDB7ZJwNB.

"John Wooden." *Wikipedia*. October 22, 2023. https://en.wikipedia.org/wiki/John_Wooden.

Kipling, Rudyard. *Rewards and Fairies*. Germany, SoftBook Press, 1910.

Comeaux, Chris, host. "Time with Quint Studer." TCN Talks Podcast. May 17, 2023. Apple Podcasts. https://podcasts.apple.com/us/podcast/time-with-quint-studer/id1550178783?i=1000613354123.

Covey, Stephen R.. *The 7 Habits of Highly Effective People: Powerful Lessons in Personal Change*. India, Simon & Schuster, 2013.

"Influence." *Merriam-Webster.com Dictionary*, Merriam-Webster, https://www.merriam-webster.com/dictionary/influence. Accessed 6 Nov. 2023.

Maxwell, John C., and Dornan, Jim. *How to Influence People: Make a Difference in Your World*. United States, HarperCollins Leadership, 2013.

Bibliography

Adelaja, Sunday. https://sundayadelajablog.com/

Buchanan, PhD, Laurie. *The Business of Being: Soul Purpose In and Out of the Workplace*. United States, She Writes Press.

The Lord of the Rings, The Fellowship of the Ring. Directed by Peter Jackson, performances by Ian McKellen, Elijah Wood, and Viggo Mortensen. New Line Cinema, WingNut Films, Marzano Films, The Saul Zaentz Company, 2001.

Shakespeare, William. *As You Like it: A Comedy*. United Kingdom, S. Gosnell, 1810.

Gordon, Jon. *The Energy Bus: 10 Rules to Fuel Your Life, Work, and Team with Positive Energy*. United Kingdom, Wiley, 2015.

"Intention becomes reality." From the writings of Janet Bull, MD, retired Chief Medical Officer of Four Seasons, 2022.

Shaw, George Bernard. "This is the true joy in life: being used for a purpose recognized by yourself as a mighty one..." Letter to a friend. 1903.

Frankl, Viktor E.. *Man's Search For Meaning*. United Kingdom, Pocket Books, 1985.

Epictetus. The Discourses of Epictetus. N.p., Phoemixx Classics Ebooks, 2021.

Waters, Patrick. From the writings of..."Catch a revelation of who you are and change will be nothing."

Chamine, Shirzad. *Positive Intelligence*. Austin, Tx: Greenleaf Book Group Press. 2016

Maslow, Abraham. *A Theory of Human Motivation*. Paper, 1943

Pericles. Speech in Thucydides' *History of the Peloponnesian War*, II.43.3.

It's a Wonderful Life. Directed by Frank Capra, performances by James Stewart, Donna Reed, and Lionel Barrymore. RKO Radio Pictures, 1946.

Heath, Chip, and Heath, Dan. *Made to Stick: Why Some Ideas Survive and Others Die.* United States, Random House Publishing Group, 2007.

Keller, Helen. Speech at a meeting of the American Association to Promote the Teaching of Speech to the Deaf, Mt. Airy, Philadelphia, Pennsylvania, July 8, 1896. https://en.wikipedia.org/wiki/Helen_Keller

Maxwell, John C.. *Quotes from John Maxwell: Insights on Leadership.* United States, B&H Publishing Group, 2014.

Madera, Chip. From the writings of... https://www.chipmadera.com/

Covey, Stephen R., et al. *First Things First.* United States, Mango Media, 2015.

Bennis, Warren. Cited in: Dianna Daniels Booher (1991) *Executive's portfolio of model speeches for all occasions.* p. 34. https://business.uc.edu/centers-partnerships/warren-bennis-leadership.html

Obama, Barack. *United States, 44th Presidential Inaugural Address,* Washington, District of Columbia, January 20, 2009

Drucker, Peter F. *The Five Most Important Questions You Will Ever Ask About Your Organization.* Germany, Wiley, 2008.

Collins, James Charles, et al. *Built to Last: Successful Habits of Visionary Companies.* United Kingdom, Century, 1995.

Studer, Quint. Roundtable Discussion: *Drive Employee Actions That Support a Culture of Belonging.* Studor Education, Huron. https://www.studereducation.com/drive-employee-actions-that-support-a-culture-of-belonging/

Bibliography

Simon Sinek's WHY Discovery Information – www.simonsinek.com

Sudden Service, mission statement. Pals. https://www.palsweb.com/

Fact, Fancy and Opinion: Examples of Present Day Writing. United States, Atlantic monthly Press, p. 215, 1923.

Omaha Bee. "Building Cathedrals." Fact, Fancy and Opinion: Examples of Present Day Writing. United States, Atlantic monthly Press, p. 215, 1923.

Harvey, Paul (host). *The Rest of the Story*, Radio Program. 1940s through May 10, 1976. https://https://en.wikipedia.org/wiki/The_Rest_of_the_Story

Kushner, Harold S.. When bad things happen to good people. United States, Schocken Books, 1989.

De Pree, Max. *Leading Without Power: Finding Hope in Serving Community*. United Kingdom, Wiley, 1997. https://depree.org/about/max/

Ramsey, Dave. From the writings of...https://www.ramseysolutions.com/

Kaplan, Dr. Jay. From the writings of... https://www.jaykaplanmd.com/

Johnson, Suzi. Former CEO of Sharp Hospice in San Diego.

Barnum, P. T. *The Art of Money Getting; Or, Golden Rules for Making Money*. N.p., CreateSpace Independent Publishing Platform, 2018.

Carter-Scott, Cherie. *If Life Is a Game, These Are the Rules: Ten Rules for Being Human as Introduced in Chicken Soup for the Soul.* United States, Harmony/Rodale, 1998.

Deming, W. Edwards. *Out of the Crisis*. United States, MIT Press, 2018.

Johnson, Clay A. *The Information Diet: A Case for Conscious Comsumption*. United States, O'Reilly Media, 2015.

"There's a Hole in My Bucket" Bergliederbüchlein (c 1700).

Liker, Jeffrey K.. *The Toyota Way: 14 Management Principles from the World's Greatest Manufacturer.* Spain, McGraw Hill LLC, 2004.

Martin, Francis. *Hung by the Tongue.* United States, F. P. M. Publications, 1995.

Inception. Directed by Christopher Nolan. Performances by Leonardo DiCaprio, Joseph Gordon-Levitt, Elliott Page. Warner Bros. Pictures. 2010.

Emerson, Ralph Waldo, and Oliver, Mary. The Essential Writings of Ralph Waldo Emerson. United Kingdom, Random House Publishing Group, 2000.

Star Trek. Created by Gene Roddenberry. Paramount. 1966 - present.

The Matrix. Direct by The Wachowskis. Performances by Keanu Reeves, Laurence Fishburne, and Carrie-Anne Moss. Warner Bros. 1999.

Brown, Brené. *Dare to Lead: Brave Work. Tough Conversations. Whole Hearts..* United States, Random House Publishing Group, 2018.

Schultz, Howard, and Gordon, Joanne. *Onward: How Starbucks Fought for Its Life Without Losing Its Soul.* United States, Rodale, 2012.

Lafley, A.G. "What Only the CEO Can Do." *Harvard Business Review,* May, 2009.

The Ghost and the Darkness. Directed by Stephen Hopkins. Performances by Michael Douglas and Val Kilmer, Paramount Pictures, 1996.

Steve Jobs. https://en.wikipedia.org/wiki/Steve_Jobs

Welch, Jack. Cited by Claudio Fernández-Aráoz in "Jack Welch's Approach to Leadership," *Harvard Business Review,* March 03, 2020. https://hbr.org/2020/03/jack-welchs-approach-to-leadership

Bibliography

Krzyzewski, Mike https://coachk.com/quotes/

Hilts, Elizabeth. *Getting in Touch with your Inner Bitch*. VDOC Pub. 2006.

Braveheart. Directed by Mel Gibson. Performances by Mel Gibson, Sophie Marceau, and Patrick McGoohan. Paramount Pictures, 1995.

Forest Gump. Directed by Robert Zemeckis. Performances by Tom Hanks, Robin Wright, Gary Sinise, and *Gladiator*. Paramount Pictures. 1994.

Gladiator. Directed by Ridley Scott. Performances by Russell Crowe, Joaquin Phoenix, and Connie Nielsen. Dreamworks Distribution. 2000.

Stanley, Andy. Pastor of North Point Community Church, https://northpoint.org/

Hoffer, Eric. The *True Believer: Thoughts on the Nature of Mass Movements*. United States, HarperCollins, 2011.

Kahl, Jack, and Donelan, Tom. *Leading from the Heart: Choosing to be a Servant Leader*. United States, Jack Kahl and Associates, 2004.

Saban, Nick. https://en.wikipedia.org/wiki/Nick_Saban

Landry, Tom. https://en.wikipedia.org/wiki/Tom_Landry

Acton Academy. https://www.actonacademy.org/.

Confucius. https://en.wikipedia.org/wiki/

Kung Fu Panda 2. Directed by Jennifer Yuh Nelson. Performances by Jack Black, Angelina Jolie, and Dustin Hoffman. Paramount Pictures. 2011.

Schwarzkopf, General Norman H. Cited by Heath Lewis. "At the Core of Credibility: Competence and Character." *CPH Blog*. https://blog.cph.org/read/ministry/credibility-competence-and-character#:~:text=Both%20competency%20and%20character%20 are%20essential%20in%20the,you%20must%20be%20without%20 one%2C%20be%20without%20strategy.%E2%80%9D

Family Ties. Created by Gary David Goldberg. Performances by Michael J. Fox, Meredith Baxter Birney, Michael Gross, 7 seasons, 176 episodes and one film. September 22, 1982 – May 14, 1989

The Andy Griffith Show. Created by Sheldon Leonard. Performances by Andy Griffith, Ron Howard, Don Knotts, 8 seasons, 249 episodes. October 3, 1960 – April 1, 1968.

Senge, Peter M. *The Fifth Discipline: The Art and Practice of the Learning Organization.* United Kingdom, Doubleday/Currency, 2006.

Amazon. https://www.amazon.com/

Avon. https://www.avon.com/

Ford. https://www.ford.com/

IBM. https://www.ibm.com/

McDonald's: https://www.mcdonalds.com/us/en-us.html

Nordstrom: https://www.nordstrom.com/

Starbucks: https://www.starbucks.com/

Gates, Bill. Business @ the Speed of Thought: Succeeding in the Digital Economy. United States, Grand Central Publishing, 2009.

United Technologies Corporation. Annual Report. https://app.stocklight.com/stocks/us/manufacturing/nyse-rtx/rtx/annual-reports/nyse-rtx-2020-10K-20580848.pdf

Lehto, Aimee and Coyner, Boyd. "Impossible is nothing" ad campaign, Adidas and TBWA, 2020.

A Preview of *It's About Time*

The Interview - The story of the day that changed my life and set me on my path to cause and purpose.

The Mountains are Calling

As I walked out of the airport in Asheville, North Carolina, in March 2002, I distinctly remember the smell of the mountain air. It was the beginning of spring, which came early that year. The scent in the air, which is imprinted indelibly on my brain to this day, was Western North Carolina Mountain pollen. Stepping off the plane, it hit me like a fragrance from heaven. I remember the grass as so green and the mountains so beautiful. It was like I had landed in one of the most beautiful places I had ever imagined.

"I Didn't Choose the Path; it chose me…"

Now, I see this all as God wooing me to His purpose, a path I never could have chosen for myself. In reality, no one grows up, at least not when I was coming up, and says, "I want to get a degree and work in hospice and be part of a team who will take part in creating this thing now known as palliative care." In fact, growing up, my hero was Michael J. Fox, who portrayed Alex Keaton on *Family Ties*. Alex was a young Reagan

Republican who wanted to be a businessman and make a lot of money. I am a bit embarrassed to admit that now, but that was me back then. No one chooses hospice work for the sole purpose of making money, and hospice as a career was not something I would necessarily have chosen as a youth. However, as many of us say in this line of work, "I didn't choose the path; the path chose me."

I convinced my wife, and myself that taking this trip was just to brush up on my interview skills. I assured her there was no way we would move to North Carolina as settled as we were in Pensacola, Florida. We had a two-year-old and a three-month-old, with my wife's family nearby to help us raise our little ones. Also, Pensacola had a beauty all its own.

However, prior to the trip, I had been getting a sense that I was being called to a change, something that would stretch me and grow me further. My first role in this career journey was as a CFO for a large Florida hospice organization, and I was beginning to feel the next step for me was hospice CEO. Coincidentally, a little hospice nestled in the mountains of western North Carolina in Hendersonville was looking for a CEO. They were a small program, so small that each branch office of the hospice where I currently worked was larger than this entire organization. I knew I would not be moving, so why did I go to the interview?

Book Review: *It's About Time*

As often happens in life, a friend put the opportunity before me. He was on the board of directors of this small hospice program. In addition to his prompting, I was getting a constant sense through quiet time and prayer that I needed a new opportunity to help me keep growing and continue my learning.

Raising the Stakes

As I traveled from Pensacola to Asheville, North Carolina, God's plan began to reveal itself in a way I never expected. I learned that a friend and professional rival was the other key candidate for the position. We ended up on the same flight, and after some interesting conversation resembling a chess match, we looked at each other with the same exclamation: "You mean you are traveling to interview for the Four Seasons position? So am I!"

I had not been invested in the position. I was just *brushing up on my interview skills*. But, suddenly, this became a competition! What can I say? I am competitive, and it is amazing what conspires to put you on the right path.

I will admit it is strange hanging out with the person you are competing with for a position. Four Seasons had us both stay in the same incredibly quaint bed and breakfast. The owner was also a board member of Four Seasons. She was a great host and made us feel so welcome. I kept getting this sense that I had arrived in the real-life Mayberry from *The Andy Griffith Show*.

"Float Like a Butterfly"

The interview day started with an early breakfast with one of the key leaders on the team. Interviews continued throughout the morning, and I began to fall in love with the team members as I discerned their vision. They had a profound sense of what their program could become with the right leader.

I later learned that a visionary board member, one of the top executives at the local bank, helped create the vision that this little hospice could become one of the best hospices in America. Frankly, this vision seemed crazy. There was nothing outwardly that would give the outward appearance that this could happen. However, that is what vision does—it casts a dream that allows intentional people to build toward the impossible.

Four Seasons showed incredible intelligence in setting up this unique interview process. They kept us away from their offices, which, at the time, were a small house and a strip of metal buildings. Instead, they held the interviews at the bank building, the tallest building in Hendersonville. It was all part of a beautifully designed process. The bank building afforded incredible views of the mountains; it was all quite enchanting. They designed everything to impress, to help punch well above their weight class

The lunch interview was a meeting with all the board members at one time and, yes, with my friendly rival. Can you imagine having two candidates in the room together at the same time over lunch? I was gracious, and my opponent was hyper-competitive, so much so that he cut in front of me right as I was about to sit at a table via invitation from two key board members who were people of influence. That gracious act of stepping aside was noticed. Years later, those board members told me that when I stepped aside and gave the other candidate my seat, it made a great impression on them.

"Sting Like a Bee"

After lunch came the big challenge. To this day, I am still astounded at the logic and ingenuity behind this interview idea. The board had both candidates go into separate rooms for thirty minutes to prepare a presentation. We had two choices to pick from, and then we had to make a full presentation to the entire Four Seasons Board of Directors. I chose the topic I did not understand, which was whether they should pursue launching a palliative care program. The palliative care program had been a huge source of debate amongst the board prior to the CEO search.

I do not remember what I said, but I made a good impression with my presentation. Looking back, I would be more nervous today giving that same presentation. Was it because I was indifferent to being selected for the position? Was it because I was young and naive? I was only thirty years old at the time. Was it because this was my cause—my destiny—and I was jumping into a stream pulling me in the direction of this opportunity? In retrospect, I know it was a bit of all those things mixed together.

Flying back to Pensacola, I became fully convinced this was something I was supposed to do. I knew a great adventure awaited me, and I remember even tearing up at the thought. I called my wife from the airport, saying, "I think this is something we are supposed to do." My lovely wife said, "I trust you. If this is something you think we are meant to do, then let's do it."

Book Review: *It's About Time*

Decision Made

That is how I became the CEO of Four Seasons in Hendersonville, North Carolina. The small hospice would later become a nationally known hospice and palliative care program, winning the American Hospital Association's Circle of Life Award twice, and receiving a ten-million-dollar grant from the Centers for Medicare and Medicaid Innovation (CMMI). The grant was to prove palliative care was necessary for the country and hopefully create a pathway for the future in how to provide and pay for the service.

The point of this story was not just to tell you how I got to Four Seasons. In fact, I first wrote this story for myself while on vacation with my family because we often forget the miracles that occur in our lives. The miracle of being the CEO of Four Seasons twice (see About the Author at the end of the book for my full background) and how it even came to pass is one of the biggest blessings of my life. The people I worked with, the people we impacted, and having a purposeful vocation that allowed me to provide for my family—what an incredible blessing it has been.

I wrote about it because, as I reflect, I realize there are so many rich lessons packed into my little story.

The Ripple Effect

The board member who first cast such a rich vision, a dream that many bought into hook, line, and sinker, was compelling. For me, his pitch seduced me to interview for a job I had no intention of taking. That is what a compelling vision will do. As I shared in my first book, *The Anatomy of Leadership*, where I quoted Peter Senge, "It is not what the vision is; it is what the vision does."

It is incredible to see the fulfillment of a vision that has touched more than ten thousand lives in western North Carolina and across the globe as we went on to establish a partnership with the country of Zambia for palliative care. Later, Four Seasons co-founded Teleios Collaborative Network, which works with hospices all over the United States. Casting a great vision is like dropping a pebble in the pond. The beautiful concentric rings traveling ever outwards show us a picture of the impact a vision can have on others in its path. *It is not what the vision is; it is what the vision does.*

Cause and Purpose

It is fundamental to truly live to seek one's cause and purpose and to be open to adventure, wherever it may take you. It was crazy for my

Book Review: *It's About Time*

wife and I to pull up roots from Pensacola and move to western North Carolina, but we knew this was where *our cause and purpose* were taking us. Indeed, it would be a great adventure, and it continues to be that adventure even to this day.

Although we knew we were being called to North Carolina, we wrestled with the decision because life does not *just all work out* like the movies. Even after that phone call to my wife from the airport, I still had to wait on an offer from Four Seasons. We also had to grapple with leaving family, finding a home, and deal with the impact of our decision as individuals and as a family.

I remember traveling back to Hendersonville with my family and my wife's dad to make our final decision. During that trip, I read this scripture:

"I lift my eyes to the mountains—where does my help come from? My help comes from the Lord, the Maker of heaven and earth." - Psalm 121:1

When I read that verse, I felt assured of two things: 1) God was indeed calling us to take this opportunity, and 2) I would need a lot of help on this great adventure. Both have proven true.

Application and Challenge

I want to challenge you by asking, "What is your cause and purpose? What has your adventure been like?" In my last book, *The Anatomy of Leadership*, I offered up a common definition of what leadership is and what leaders do. In this book, we will give you the *7 Fundamentals* to live your cause and purpose daily.

Stop now and use the space provided. Draw if you want to draw, write if you want to write. Do not try to edit it, and do not force it. What have you been created to do? There may be several things. Take a deep breath, let it out, and take this space to capture what comes to you.

Taking the role of CEO at Four Seasons, in many respects, was the beginning of my leadership journey and the beginning of the quest to find and live my cause and purpose. I am closing in on thirty years

_____

_____

_____

_____

Book Review: *It's About Time*

of working in hospice and palliative care. I am now the CEO of Teleios Collaborative Network (Teleios) and Teleios Consulting Group (Teleios). In both positions, I do leadership coaching, training, speaking, and strategic planning, and I have come to find one of my purposes is to help other people find theirs. One of my other purposes is to help people live their purpose. I am convinced that your purpose, whatever it is, comes down to leadership. In my last book, I defined what leadership is, and this book is to help you live it daily.

May the adventure begin…and continue…

About the Author

**Chris Comeaux, CPA, MLAS
President/CEO Teleios
Collaborative Network and
Teleios Consulting Group
ccomeaux@teleioscn.org**

Chris Comeaux (KO-mo) is an award-winning expert and lifelong student of leadership and the performance required to be a true leader. He has spent his life and career researching, learning, coaching, and implementing the pushes and pulls necessary to create high-performance leaders and organizations.

Chris is the President/CEO of Teleios Collaborative Network (TCN), a collaboration founded by Four Seasons Compassion for Life, Carolina Caring, AMOREM, and Mountain Valley Hospice & Palliative Care. TCN is fourteen members strong, reaching across eight states. TCN has been named by Modern Healthcare as one of America's Best Places to Work in 2023, 2022, and 2021, and was #2 in the nation in 2021. The goal of TCN's collaboration is to harness the best of each hospice and enable the network to care for the patients and families in each community served. TCN introduces innovations across the membership network and works with payors on creative solutions for those dealing with serious and advanced illnesses.

Over the years, Chris has become nationally known as a leader in our country's hospice and palliative care industry. He has spent a substantial portion of his career as President/CEO of Four Seasons in western North Carolina, a two-time American Hospital Association Circle of Life Award Winner. In 2005, the Carolinas Center for Hospice and End of Life Care honored him with the Peter Keese Leadership Award.

In 2006, Chris left Four Seasons for two years to build an alliance between the prestigious national healthcare consulting firm, the Studer Group, and Covenant Hospice in Pensacola. The vision was to transform, develop, and grow leaders throughout the hospice and palliative care world. Chris grew this venture from its infancy to an established coaching firm that partnered with post-acute healthcare organizations from New York to California. He returned to Four Seasons in 2008 to apply what he learned about leadership in the trenches to an organization he knew and loved.

About the Author

In 2020, Chris helped co-found Teleios Consulting Group (TCG), a coaching and consulting company that applies the leadership principles used in TCN and the leadership system Chris has developed for clients all over the US. Chris believes, "If the principles and tools we teach work in hospice and palliative care, they will work in any business."

Chris's hospice career began in 1997 at Covenant Hospice in Pensacola, Florida. Earlier in his career, he worked with KPMG Peat Marwick, a "Big Four" CPA consulting firm. He also worked in the Executive Development Program of Cooper Industries, a Fortune 100 Company.

Chris has a Master in Leadership from The Thayer Institute.

Chris is married to Deshia, and they are the proud parents of five children (three boys and two girls). Chris enjoys spending time outdoors with his family, reading, learning, and hiking in the mountains of Western North Carolina.

www.ingramcontent.com/pod-product-compliance
Lightning Source LLC
Chambersburg PA
CBHW050854160426
43194CB00011B/2155